AN EXCERPT FROM
THE GOSPEL ACCORDING TO

MATTHEW 1

(CHAPTER 6:5-24)

THE PREACHER'S OUTLINE & SERMON BIBLE®

New Testament

King James
Version

Leadership Ministries Worldwide
Chattanooga, TN
www.lmw.org • info@lmw.org

The Preacher's Outline & Sermon Bible® is written for God's people to use in their preparation for preaching and teaching. Leadership Ministries Worldwide wants God's people to use *The Preacher's Outline & Sermon Bible*®. The purpose of the copyright is to prevent the reproduction, misuse, and abuse of the material.

May our Lord bless us all as we preach, teach, and write for Him, fulfilling His great commission to make disciples of all nations.

Please address all requests for information or permission to:
Leadership Ministries Worldwide
1928 Central Avenue
Chattanooga, TN 37408
Ph.# (423) 855-2181   FAX (423) 855-8616   E-Mail info@lmw.org
http://www.lmw.org

Library of Congress Catalog Card Number: 96-75921
International Standard Book Number:
978-1-57407-293-8

Printed in the United States of America

1   2   3   4   5   10   11   12   13   14

LEADERSHIP MINISTRIES WORLDWIDE

DEDICATED

To all the men and women of the world who
preach and teach the Gospel of
our Lord Jesus Christ and
to the Mercy and Grace of God

&

- Demonstrated to us in Christ Jesus our Lord.

    *In him we have redemption through his
    blood, the forgiveness of sins, in accord-
    ance with the riches of God's grace.
    (Ep.1:7)*

- Out of the mercy and grace of God, His Word has
flowed. Let every person know that God will have
mercy upon him, forgiving and using him to fulfill
His glorious plan of salvation.

    *For God so loved the world that he gave
    his one and only Son, that whoever be-
    lieves in him shall not perish but have
    eternal life. For God did not send his Son
    into the world to condemn the world, but to
    save the world through him. (Jn.3:16-17)*

    *This is good, and pleases God our Savior,
    who wants all men to be saved and to come
    to a knowledge of the truth. (1 Ti.2:3-4)*

10/07

The Preacher's Outline & Sermon Bible®

is written for God's
servants to use in their
study, teaching, and
preaching of God's Holy
Word...

- to share the Word of God
with the world.
- to help believers, both ministers and laypersons, in
their understanding, preaching, and teaching of God's
Word.
- to do everything we possi-
bly can to lead men, women,
boys, and girls to give their
hearts and lives to Jesus
Christ and to secure the
eternal life that He offers.
- to do all we can to minister
to the needy of the world.
- to give Jesus Christ His
proper place, the place the
Word gives Him. Therefore,
no work of Leadership Ministries Worldwide—no Out-
line Bible Resources—will
ever be personalized.

ACKNOWLEDGMENTS AND BIBLIOGRAPHY

Every child of God is precious to the LORD and deeply loved. And every child as a servant of the LORD touches the lives of those who come in contact with him or his ministry. The writing ministries of the following servants have touched this work, and we are grateful that God brought their writings our way. We hereby acknowledge their ministry to us, being fully aware that there are so many others down through the years whose writings have touched our lives and who deserve mention, but whose names have faded from our memory. May our wonderful LORD continue to bless the ministries of these dear servants—and the ministries of us all—as we diligently labor to reach the world for Christ and to meet the desperate needs of those who suffer so much.

THE GREEK SOURCES

1. *Expositor's Greek Testament*, Edited by W. Robertson Nicoll. Grand Rapids, MI: Eerdmans Publishing Co., 1970

2. Robertson, A.T. *Word Pictures in the New Testament*. Nashville, TN: Broadman Press, 1930.

3. Thayer, Joseph Henry. *Greek-English Lexicon of the New Testament*. New York: American Book Co, No date listed.

4. Vincent, Marvin R. *Word Studies in the New Testament*. Grand Rapids, MI: Eerdmans Publishing Co., 1969.

5. Vine, W.E. *Expository Dictionary of New Testament Words*. Old Tappan, NJ: Fleming H. Revell Co. No date listed.

6. Wuest, Kenneth S. *Word Studies in the Greek New Testament*. Grand Rapids, MI: Eerdmans Publishing Co., 1966.

THE REFERENCE WORKS

7. *Cruden's Complete Concordance of the Old & New Testament*. Philadelphia, PA: The John C. Winston Co., 1930.

8. Josephus' *Complete Works*. Grand Rapids, MI: Kregel Publications, 1981.

9. Lockyer, Herbert. Series of Books, including his Books on *All the Men, Women, Miracles, and Parables of the Bible*. Grand Rapids, MI: Zondervan Publishing House, 1958-1967.

10. -*Nave's Topical Bible*. Nashville, TN: The Southwestern Co., No date listed.

11. *The Amplified New Testament*. (Scripture Quotations are from the Amplified New Testament, Copyright 1954, 1958, 1987 by the Lockman Foundation. Used by permission.)

12. *The Four Translation New Testament* (Including King James, New American Standard, Williams - New Testament In the Language of the People, Beck - New Testament In the Language of Today.) Minneapolis, MN: World Wide Publications.

13. *The New Compact Bible Dictionary*, Edited by T. Alton Bryant. Grand Rapids, MI: Zondervan Publishing House, 1967.

14. *The New Thompson Chain Reference Bible*. Indianapolis, IN: B.B. Kirkbride Bible Co., 1964,

THE COMMENTARIES

15. Barclay, William. *Daily Study Bible Series*. Philadelphia, PA: Westminster Press, Began in 1953.

16. Bruce, F.F. *The Epistle to the Ephesians*. Westwood, NJ: Fleming H. Revell Co., 1968.

17. Bruce, F.F. *Epistle to the Hebrews*. Grand Rapids, MI: Eerdmans Publishing Co., 1964.

18. Bruce, F.F. *The Epistles of John*. Old Tappan, NJ: Fleming H. Revell Co., 1970.

19. Criswell, W.A. *Expository Sermons on Revelation*. Grand Rapids, MI: Zondervan Publishing House, 1962-66.

20. Greene, Oliver. *The Epistles of John*. Greenville, SC: The Gospel Hour, Inc., 1966.

21. Greene, Oliver. *The Epistles of Paul the Apostle to the Hebrews*. Greenville, SC: The Gospel Hour, Inc., 1965.

22. Greene, Oliver. *The Epistles of Paul the Apostle to Timothy & Titus*. Greenville, SC: The Gospel Hour, Inc., 1964.

23. Greene, Oliver. *The Revelation Verse by Verse Study*. Greenville, SC: The Gospel Hour, Inc., 1963.

24. Henry, Matthew. *Commentary on the Whole Bible*. Old Tappan, NJ: Fleming H. Revell Co.

25. Hodge, Charles. *Exposition on Romans & on Corinthians*. Grand Rapids, MI: Eerdmans Publishing Co., 1972-1973.

26. Ladd, George Eldon. *A Commentary On the Revelation of John*. Grand Rapids, MI: Eerdmans Publishing Co., 1972-1973.

27. Leupold, H.C. *Exposition of Daniel*. Grand Rapids, MI: Baker Book House, 1969.

28. Morris, Leon. *The Gospel According to John*. Grand Rapids, MI: Eerdmans Publishing Co., 1971.

29. Newell, William R. *Hebrews, Verse by Verse*. Chicago, IL: Moody Press, 1947.

ACKNOWLEDGMENTS AND BIBLIOGRAPHY

30. Strauss, Lehman. *Devotional Studies in Galatians & Ephesians*. Neptune, NJ: Loizeaux Brothers, 1957.

31. Strauss, Lehman. *Devotional Studies in Philippians*. Neptune, NJ: Loizeaux Brothers, 1959.

32. Strauss, Lehman. *James, Your Brother*. Neptune, NJ: Loizeaux Brothers, 1956.

33. Strauss, Lehman. *The Book of the Revelation*. Neptune, NJ: Loizeaux Brothers, 1964.

34. *The New Testament & Wycliffe Bible Commentary*, Edited by Charles F. Pfeiffer & Everett F. Harrison. New York: The Iverson Associates, 1971. Produced for Moody Monthly. Chicago Moody Press, 1962.

35. *The Pulpit Commentary*, Edited by H.D.M. Spence & Joseph S. Exell. Grand Rapids, MI: Eerdmans Publishing Co., 1950.

36. Thomas, W.H. Griffith. *Hebrews, A Devotional Commentary*. Grand Rapids, MI: Eerdmans Publishing Co., 1970.

37. Thomas, W.H. Griffith. *Outline Studies in the Acts of the Apostles*. Grand Rapids, MI: Eerdmans Publishing Co., 1956.

38. Thomas, W.H. Griffith. *St. Paul's Epistle to the Romans*. Grand Rapids, MI: Eerdmans Publishing Co., 1946.

39. Thomas, W.H. Griffith. *Studies in Colossians & Philemon*. Grand Rapids, MI: Baker Book House, 1973.

40. *Tyndale New Testament Commentaries*. Grand Rapids, MI: Eerdmans Publishing Co., Began in 1958.

41. Walker, Thomas. *Acts of the Apostles*. Chicago, IL: Moody Press, 1965.

42. Walvoord, John. *The Thessalonian Epistles*. Grand Rapids, MI: Zondervan Publishing House, 1973.

"Woe is unto me, if I preach not the gospel"
(1 Co.9:16)

	L. The Right Motive for Prayer, DS1,2,3 6:5-6

1. The wrong motive: Praying to be seen by men
  a. The place: Loving to pray in the synagogue & in the streets
  b. The reason: For recognition, to be seen as holy
  c. The reward: People's esteem
2. The right motive: Praying to be heard by God
  a. The location: In one's private place
  b. The reason: God is in one's secret or private place*DS4*
  c. The reward: Will be heard & blessed by God
	5 And when thou prayest, thou shalt not be as the hypocrites are: for they love to pray standing in the synagogues and in the corners of the streets, that they may be seen of men. Verily I say unto you, They have their reward.
	6 But thou, when thou prayest, enter into thy closet, and when thou hast shut thy door, pray to thy Father which is in secret; and thy Father which seeth in secret shall reward thee openly.

DIVISION IV

THE TEACHINGS OF THE MESSIAH TO HIS DISCIPLES: THE GREAT SERMON ON THE MOUNT, 5:1–7:29

L.   The Right Motive for Prayer (Part I), 6:5-6

(6:5-6) **Introduction—Prayer—Motive**: this passage is speaking to *those who pray*—people who take prayer seriously. Prayer is one of the greatest acts of the Christian believer. Talking to God, whether by thought or tongue, is the way a believer fellowships with God; and the one thing God desires is fellowship with man (Is.43:10). Thus, it is essential that we pray and pray often, sharing all day long.

However, that we *do* pray is not the concern of Christ in this point. His concern is *how* we pray. It is possible to pray amiss, with the wrong motive and in the wrong way. It is possible to pray and never be heard by God. It is possible to pray and to be speaking only to ourselves, to have our prayer go no higher than our own ears. Therefore, Christ sets out to teach us the right and wrong motives for praying.

  1. The wrong motive: praying to be seen by men (v.5).
  2. The right motive: praying to be heard by God (v.6).

DEEPER STUDY # 1

(6:5-8) **Prayer**: there are dangers surrounding prayer, some negative factors that must be guarded against.

  1. Prayer can become hypocritical (v.5). A person can pray for the wrong reasons, with the wrong motives.

  2. Prayer can become habit-forming (v.5). Prayer is a wonderful experience, very rewarding emotionally and mentally and in having our needs met as God answers our prayer. We can begin to *love praying* and still be praying amiss.

  3. Prayer can become connected with certain places (v.5). A believer has places that mean much to him in his prayer life, but he must guard against limiting God's presence only to those places, even if it is the church.

  4. Prayer can become empty repetition (v.7). A person can take any phrase or form of prayer and make it a meaningful experience, or make it a formal and meaningless occasion. (Note how often the Lord's Prayer is repeated by rote memory with the mind focused elsewhere.)

  5. Prayer can become too long (v.7). A believer can begin to feel he is heard because of "much speaking" (see Ecc.5:1-2).

  6. Prayer can become self-glorifying (v.8). A person can begin to feel he must inform and convince God of his *great* need. When the answer comes (out of the mercy of God, despite praying amiss), the believer begins to *glory in his spirituality*—that he has what it takes to get things from God.

  7. Prayer can become self-deceptive (vv.7-8). A person can begin to think he is heard (1) because of *much speaking* and (2) because he convinces God of his need.

DEEPER STUDY # 2

(6:5-6) **Prayer**: note several things.

  1. Christ says "When thou prayest." He is referring to personal prayer (see v.6).

  2. Christ assumes that the believer does pray, and the idea conveyed is that the believer prays often.

  3. Christ says there is a right way and a wrong way to pray. "When thou prayest, thou shalt not...." vs. "But thou, when thou prayest...."

  4. Christ says that some "love to pray," and they are the very ones who commit this fault. They pray amiss, with the wrong motive.

  5. Christ pictures two men praying. One man prays to men (v.5); the other man prays to the Father (v.6). The first man is a hypocrite; the second man is a true son of the Father.

DEEPER STUDY # 3

(6:5-6) **Prayer**: believers are expected to pray. Prayer is God's appointed medium through which He acts for man. *Sharing and talking* together is the way all persons communicate, fellowship, and commune together. This is true both with men and God. Prayer requires our presence, sharing, and talking; and God wants to fellowship and commune with us. Few persons heed this fact; few persons take prayer seriously. Therefore, if we want the blessings of God upon our lives and ministries—if we want the work of God going forth in power and bearing fruit—we must pray and we must intercede in prayer.

> "Pray to thy Father" (Mt.6:6; see Mt.6:7).
> "After this manner pray ye" (Mt.6:9).
> "Pray ye the Lord of the harvest" (Mt.9:38; Lu.10:2).
> "Watch and pray that ye enter not into temptation" (Mt.26:41; Mk.13:33; 14:38; Lu.21:36; 22:40, 46).
> "Men ought always to pray, and not to faint" (Lu.18:1).
> "Praying always with all prayer and supplication in the Spirit, and watching thereunto with all perseverance and supplication for all saints" (Ep.6:18).
> "Pray without ceasing" (1 Th.5:17).
> "I will that men pray everywhere" (1 Ti.2:8).

1 (6:5) **Prayer—Motive**: the wrong motive for prayer is praying to be seen by men. Two preliminary things need to be looked at before discussing this point.

a. Praying—even loving to pray—is not a sign that a person really knows God.

b. The fact that a person really knows God means that he does pray. No matter what a man may think in his mind, if he really knows God and really believes in God, he talks to God. There is nothing that could keep him from praying. He knows God personally—knows Him as his Father who loves and cares for him ever so deeply. Therefore, just as any child who truly loves his father, the believer talks, converses, and shares with his Father.

This says something to the person who prays primarily in public and prays little, if any, in private. He must search the genuineness of his heart and profession.

Christ says that a man who prays to be seen by men *loves to pray, but he is a hypocrite*.

a. The places where he *loves* to pray are *out in public*, in the synagogue (church), and in the streets (restaurants and other public places).

Thought 1. Note five lessons.

(1) Some love to pray publicly. They love representing the group and vocalizing their praise and needs to God. Some have become very charismatic and fluent at public prayer, yet they lack that essential love for private praying. Christ says, "hypocrite" (v.5).

(2) Some pray only in public. They pray before their family (at meals and family prayers, usually with children); in church (when called upon); and in public (when eating in restaurants). They seldom, if ever, pray in private. How destitute is the prayer life of so many!

(3) Prayer is to be offered to God both in church and in public. But public prayer is to be public, not private. Too often a person has his *personal devotions* when called upon to pray publicly. He has neglected his *private prayers* and his inner need has not been met. Thus when he begins to pray publicly, he slips into praying his own *private prayer* instead of representing the group.

(4) Some hypocrites pray, and they pray much. There are some *religious people* who pray little, if any. These can learn from the hypocrites.

(5) Note the posture of this hypocrite. He stood praying. This is an acceptable posture for prayer (Mk.11:25); but the picture is that of pride, arrogance, and self-confidence. Kneeling is a picture of humility, reverence, and dependence upon God (Lu.22:41; Ep.3:14).

> "Be of the same mind one toward another, Mind not high things, but condescend to men of low estate. Be not wise in your own conceits" (Ro.12:16).
> "For if a man think himself to be something, when he is nothing, he deceiveth himself" (Ga.6:3).
> "For all that is in the world, the lust of the flesh, and the lust of the eyes, and the pride of life, is not of the Father, but is of the world" (1 Jn.2:16).
> "Behold, his soul which is lifted up is not upright in him: but the just shall live by his faith" (Hab.2:4).

b. The man who prays only in public prays for only one reason: not because he loves to pray but because he loves recognition.

Thought 1. Note two lessons.

(1) The sin is not failing to pray. The sin is praying *only* in church and in public. A person who prays publicly but seldom prays privately fools himself. Christ says real prayer (prayer to the Father) matters nothing to that person. He prays only for recognition—to be heard by men.

(2) Praying publicly should be done. There is a great danger, however, in public prayer: having one's pride stroked. It is so easy to be praying publicly and have self-centered thoughts run across one's mind....

- that one is really praying a good prayer. Such prayer is nothing but waxing eloquent with words
- that one's prayer will surely be admired
- that one's prayer is really demonstrating a close walk with God (a deep spirituality)

"Ye hypocrites, well did Esaias prophesy of you, saying, this people draweth nigh unto me with their mouth, and honoureth me with their lips; but their heart is far from me" (Mt.15:7-8).

"And if any man think that he knoweth any thing, he knoweth nothing yet as he ought to know" (1 Co.8:2).

"When pride cometh, then cometh shame: but with the lowly is wisdom" (Pr.11:2).

"Pride goeth before destruction, and a haughty spirit before a fall" (Pr.16:18).

"Woe unto them that are wise in their own eyes, and prudent in their own sight!" (Is.5:21).

c. The man who prays only in public receives his reward: public recognition. Three things need to be clearly seen about this man.

1) He will experience good feelings and satisfying thoughts about his spiritual state and religious piety. He will possess a good self-image and some confidence in his standing with God. The esteem and praise of men and feeling good about what he has done gives him a good self image. *But* in this case it is a false self-image.

2) He has cheated himself, really missed out on the most intimate presence and greatest future in the universe. He has lost his soul. He shall never hear, "Well done thou good and faithful servant" (Mt.25:21).

3) He gets just what he deserves: public recognition. If he places so little value upon sharing with God Himself, he deserves no more than what man can give him—human recognition.

Thought 1. Man's esteem fails at several points.

(1) Man's esteem is temporary. Everything passes—ever so quickly. Man soon forgets and moves on to other things.

(2) Man's esteem becomes commonplace. Even the greatest skills that elicit praise become routine and commonplace to man when performed day by day. Soon man no longer acknowledges his uniqueness. Such abilities are merely expected and accepted; he no longer elicits praise and recognition.

(3) Man's esteem is powerless. It cannot answer prayer; it can only recognize man's ability to put words together and to see man's expression, fervency, and emotion. Its power is limited to the things of this world, and that power is even limited and short lived. Man's esteem can do absolutely nothing about the spiritual needs of his heart.

(4) Man's esteem is not to be the judge of his life—God is. No man is any greater than any other man; men are mere men. All men have the same need: to turn to God in prayer, praying for His acceptance and recognition. Therefore, the esteem of man *by men* is meaningless in light of judgment and eternity.

"For all flesh is as grass, and all the glory of man as the flower of grass. The grass withereth, and the flower thereof falleth away" (1 Pe.1:24).

"Nevertheless man being in honour abideth not: he is like the beasts that perish" (Ps.49:12).

"For when he dieth he shall carry nothing away: his glory shall not descend after him" (Ps.49:17).

"As they were increased, so they sinned against me: therefore will I change their glory into shame" (Ho.4:7).

2 (6:6) **Prayer—Motive:** the right motive for prayer is praying to be heard by God. Three preliminary things need to be looked at in this point.

1. The willingness to take time to pray: "When thou prayest." There has to be the will to pray. The believer must take time to get alone to pray. Too few ever take time to pray, and even fewer spend more than a few minutes in prayer. Too many stay all wrapped up in the world and its day-to-day affairs, some of which are necessary, but how much more necessary is prayer!

2. A closet is a necessity. The believer must have a private place deliberately chosen for prayer.

3. A personal relationship with God: a *Father-son* relationship is absolutely essential. God is our *Father*; He is available as fathers are available to their children. We are to go to Him in prayer, sharing and communing with Him. We are to allow Him to shower us with His care and protection, meeting our every need (Ps.91:1).

Note: Christ says that a man who is genuine prays to be heard by God and not by men.

a. The place he chooses for prayer is in his private closet. Christ says: "Get alone"; "Enter your closet...shut your door." Be unobserved, undisturbed, and unheard. (See 2 K.4:33; Is.26:20.)

1) *Get alone:* unobserved—out of everyone's sight.

2) *Get alone:* undisturbed—avoid interruptions and disturbances.

3) *Get alone:* unheard—concentrate and meditate to allow God the freedom to work in your heart as He wishes.

"On the morrow, as they went on their journey, and drew nigh unto the city, Peter went up upon the housetop to pray about the sixth hour" (Ac.10:9).

"And Cornelius said, Four days ago I was fasting until this hour; and at the ninth hour I prayed in my house, and, behold, a man stood before me in bright clothing" (Ac.10:30).

"But thou, when thou prayest, enter into thy closet, and when thou hast shut thy door, pray to thy Father which is in secret; and thy Father which seeth in secret shall reward thee openly" (Mt.6:6).

"**And in the morning, rising up a great while before day, he went out, and departed into a solitary place, and there prayed**" (Mk.1:35).

"**And when he had sent them away, he departed into a mountain to pray. And when even was come, the ship was in the midst of the sea, and he alone on the land**" (Mk.6:46-47).

"**And it came to pass in those days, that he went out into a mountain to pray, and continued all night in prayer to God**" (Lu.6:12).

"**And he was withdrawn from them about a stone's cast, and kneeled down, and prayed. Saying, Father, if thou be willing, remove this cup from me: nevertheless, not my will, but thine, be done**" (Lu.22:41-42).

b. The reason the believer prays in his private closet is because God is in secret (see note—Mt.6:4). Note two significant facts.

1) God *is in secret;* therefore, a person can meet God only *in secret.* Even in the midst of a worshipping crowd, a person must concentrate and focus his attention upon God who is unseen. There must be a secret heart-to-heart meeting and communion if a person wishes to pray and truly share with God.

2) God *is in secret;* therefore, He is not interested in show, but in substance. Show is before men. Substance is found in the secret, quiet, meditative place. Remember: everything that exists began with an idea, and the development of the idea came from *private and quiet thought and meditation,* not out in the public before people—at least not often. The same is true of spiritual matters. Spiritual show takes place before people, but spiritual substances or qualities that really matter take place in secret. When the believer pours out his heart, he receives his greatest encouragement and strength in the secret place of the Most High, not in the public places of mere man.

Thought 1. Many pray on the run; few pray *in secret.* Why do so few have a quiet time, a daily worship and devotional time? Why do so few keep their daily appointment with God? This is one of the most difficult things in the world to understand in light of who God is and in light of man's desperate plight and need. No man would ever fail to keep his appointment with the state leader of his nation.

(1) Many say they do not have the time, so they do not take the time. But in all honesty, it takes only a little effort to get up a while earlier in the morning—if they are really all that pressed for time. All they need to do is to rearrange their schedule to allow for a quiet time just as they arrange for any other important meeting. However, few do this; therefore, they are without excuse. Many believers are faithful in meeting God daily. It is just a matter of discipline and priority.

(2) Most have the time; they just do not take the time. They neglect getting alone with God consistently.

(3) Many have not been taught the importance and benefit of a quiet time with God every day. This is a justified accusation against Christian parents, preachers, and teachers. So few have practiced and stressed what they have always heard about the importance of prayer. The silence of believers and their failure to reach the world in sound doctrine is unbelievable, especially after two thousand years.

(4) Some have not yet learned to discipline themselves and to be consistent in their spiritual lives. There is no better area to learn discipline and consistency than in a daily quiet time. A person should just begin and do it. When a day is missed, a person should flee discouragement, "forgetting those things which are behind" and reach forth to a new day and begin again. Eventually, consistency and discipline will be learned, and the person's soul will be fed with the "unsearchable riches of Christ" (Ep.3:8, 20; see Ph.3:13).

c. The reward of the genuine prayer warrior is open blessings. The praying believer will be rewarded in two very special ways.

1) The strength and presence of God will be upon his life (Ezr.8:22; 1 Pe.5:6). God's presence is unmistakable. There is a difference between a person who walks in God's presence and a person who walks only in this world (Mt.6:25-34, esp.33).

God rewards the praying believer with His presence and blessings. The believer's needs, material and spiritual, are met day by day.

2) The believer's prayers will also be answered (Mt.21:22; Jn.16:24; 1 Jn.5:14-15). The answers to prayer are clearly seen by a thinking and honest observer. God has promised to answer the true prayer of a genuine believer. God takes care of the genuine believer with a very special care. Sometimes the answer is seen...

- in a renewed strength

"**Now unto him that is able to do exceeding abundantly above all that we ask or think, according to the power that worketh in us**" (Ep.3:20).

- in a provision of some necessity

"**But seek ye first the kingdom of God, and his righteousness; and all these things shall be added unto you**" (Mt.6:33).

- in a conquest of some great temptation or trial

"**There hath no temptation taken you but such as is common to man: but God is faithful, who will not suffer you to be tempted above that ye are able; but will with the temptation also make a way to escape, that ye may be able to bear it**" (1 Co.10:13).

- in a peace that passes all human understanding

> **"Be careful for nothing; but in every thing by prayer and supplication with thanksgiving let your request be made known unto God. And the peace of God, which passeth all understanding, shall keep your hearts and minds through Christ Jesus" (Ph.4:6-7).**

- in a soundness of mind that is incomprehensible

> **"For God hath not given us the spirit of fear; but of power, and of love, and of a sound mind" (2 Ti.1:7).**

Thought 1. The praying believer, the believer who becomes a true intercessor, will be rewarded openly on that special day of redemption.
(1) God "wonders that there [is] no man, and...no intercessor" (Is.59:16).
(2) Christ, the Great Intercessor, "ever liveth to make intercession for them" (He.7:25).
(3) The interceding believer shall stand openly in a very special relationship with Jesus, the Great Intercessor Himself, before God the Father.

> **"And all things, whatsoever ye shall ask in prayer, believing, ye shall receive" (Mt.21:22).**
> **"And I say unto you, Ask, and it shall be given you; seek, and ye shall find; knock, and it shall be opened unto you" (Lu.11:9).**
> **"And whatsoever ye shall ask in my name, that will I do, that the Father may be glorified in the Son. If ye shall ask any thing in my name, I will do it" (Jn.14:13-14).**
> **"If ye abide in me, and my words abide in you, ye shall ask what ye will, and it shall be done unto you" (Jn.15:7).**
> **"Hitherto have ye asked nothing in my name: ask, and ye shall receive, that your joy may be full" (Jn.16:24).**
> **"And whatsoever we ask, we receive of him, because we keep his commandments, and do those things that are pleasing in his sight" (1 Jn.3:22).**
> **"And this is the confidence that we have in him, that, if we ask any thing according to his will, he heareth us: and if we know that he hear us, whatsoever we ask, we know that we have the petitions that we desired of him" (1 Jn.5:14-15).**

DEEPER STUDY # 4
(6:6) **Prayer**: "Your Father is in secret...." *Secret* means three things.
  1. Concentration: meditation, contemplation, thinking deeply upon God and sharing accordingly.
  2. Apart from all: secluded, alone, private, out of view from all.
  3. Unseen: invisible, yet there; believing and having faith that God is there; spiritual, but still hearing and responding.
Every believer should have a secret, quiet place that is dear to his heart, dear because it is the place where he draws near to God and God draws near to him. (See DEEPER STUDY # 3—Jn.1:48.)

	M. The Three Great Rules for Prayer, 6:7-8
1. Rule 1: Do not use meaning-less repetition[DS1]	7 But when ye pray, use not vain repetitions, as the heathen *do:* for they think that they shall be heard for their much speaking.
2. Rule 2: Do not speak much	

3. Rule 3: Trust God
  a. He knows your needs
  b. He desires to hear your prayer
	8 Be not ye therefore like unto them: for your Father knoweth what things ye have need of, before ye ask him.

DIVISION IV

THE TEACHINGS OF THE MESSIAH TO HIS DISCIPLES: THE GREAT SERMON ON THE MOUNT, 5:1–7:29

M. The Three Great Rules for Prayer (Part II), 6:7-8

(6:7-8) **Introduction**: among the religious there is often a tendency toward long prayers, particularly in public. Too often people measure prayer by its fluency and length, thinking that length means devotion. "Be not rash with thy mouth, and let not thine heart be hasty to utter anything before God; for God is in heaven, and thou upon earth; therefore let thy words be few" (Ec.5:2). Christ puts the matter very simply, yet strongly: "When ye pray," follow three great rules.

1. Rule 1: do not use meaningless repetition (v.7).
2. Rule 2: do not speak much (v.7).
3. Rule 3: trust God (v.8).

1 (6:7) **Prayer—Repetition**: the first great rule of prayer is striking—do not use empty repetition (see Deeper Study # 1—Mt.6:7). There are several things that lend themselves to empty repetition.

a. Memorized prayer: just saying the words of a form prayer, for example, the Lord's prayer. There is nothing wrong with praying a memorized prayer, but it should be prayed through and not just repeated with no thought behind the words.

b. Written, well-worded prayers: thinking that what we say is so expressive and so well worded that it is bound to carry weight with God. The words may be descriptive and beautifully arranged, but the heart must be offering the prayer, not the mind and ego. Such prayer is empty repetition.

c. Ritual prayer: saying the same prayer at the same time on the same occasion—over and over again. This can soon become empty repetition.

d. Formal worship: praying in the same way on a rigid schedule can lead to praying by habit (repeated practice) with little or no meaning to it.

e. Thoughtless prayer: speaking words while our minds are wandering. Being tired is no excuse. It is better not to pray than to pray insincerely.

f. Religious words and phrases: using certain words or phrases over and over in prayer (just because they are religious sounding). (Compare using such words over and over as *mercy, grace, I thank thee O God, in Jesus' name.*)

g. Habitual references to God: using such empty repetition as "Lord this," and "Lord that," and "Lord here," and "Lord there," and "Lord...," "Lord...," "Lord...." How little thought is really given to approaching Him whose name is "Wonderful, Counselor, The Mighty God, The Everlasting Father, The Prince of Peace" (Is.9:6).

There are several things that will keep us from using empty repetition in prayer.
1. A genuine heart: really knowing God personally and having a moment-by-moment fellowship with Him all day long.
2. Thought and concentration: really focusing upon what we are saying.
3. Desire for fellowship with God: praying sincerely, really meaning it.
4. Preparation: preparing ourselves for prayer by first meditating in God's Word.

Note something of extreme importance in discussing *vain repetition.* Christ does not say repetition in prayer is wrong. It is not wrong. What is wrong is vain, empty, meaningless, foolish repetition. Christ Himself used repetition in prayer (Mt.26:44), so did Daniel (Da.9:18-19), and so did the Psalmist (Ps.136:1f).

Thought 1. Note six lessons.
(1) There is one major problem with the praying of believers: they do not pray enough. They do not take enough time to pray and to pray in earnest.

There is one major problem *when believers do pray*: prayer is often vain, empty, thoughtless, meaningless, and repetitive. Too often a believer prays and does not concentrate. His mind wanders off somewhere else; he only mouths the words. Such thoughtless and meaningless prayer is clearly seen in public prayer and in the powerlessness of believers today.

6

(2) There is one sure way to prepare our hearts for prayer: meditating in God's Word.

"All Scripture is given by inspiration of God, and is profitable for doctrine, for reproof, for correction, for instruction in righteousness" (2 Ti.3:16).

It is in the Scripture that the believer learns about God, himself, and the world—the nature and truth of all things. It is the Spirit of God who takes the Word of God and moves upon the believer's heart revealing that for which the believer should pray. Therefore, the believer is stirred to pray for whatever the Word of God and the Spirit of God has shown him (Ro.8:26; see Jn.14:26; 16:13; 1 Co.2:12-13).

(3) Vain repetition in prayer, whether formal or thoughtless, is *desensitizing*.
⇒ It discourages the sincere and the newly converted.
⇒ It cools the willing and the gifted.
⇒ It stifles the committed and the mature.
⇒ It turns away the seeking and the lost.

(4) Repetition in prayer *is* dull. Empty repetition affects worship, interest, and attendance at services.
(5) Vain repetition is tragic. Prayer should be one of the most meaningful experiences in life. God is certainly willing to meet the believer in a very special way—anytime, anyplace. So many hearts are just...

• barren	• dry	• desert-like
• dull	• hard	• rusted
• complacent	• lethargic	• still

So much praying is merely going over and over the same things ranging from "bless Mom and Dad" to "give us a good day tomorrow."
(6) Empty repetition turns God away and cuts the heart of the committed.

"Having a form of godliness [long prayers], but denying the power thereof: from such turn away" (2 Ti.3:5).
"Ye hypocrites, well did Esaias prophesy of you, saying, this people draweth nigh unto me with their mouth, and honoureth me with their lips; but their heart is far from me" (Mt.15:7-8).

DEEPER STUDY # 1
(6:7) **Prayer—Repetition, Vain** (battologesete): to babble much; to use many phrases; to say idle things; to say meaningless things. Vain repetition means at least two things.
1. It means saying the same words over and over again without putting one's heart and thought into what is being said.
2. It means using certain religious words or phrases (sometimes over and over again) and thinking God hears because one is using such religious talk.

---

2 (6:7) **Prayer, Long**: the second great rule of prayer is an eye-opener—do not speak much. Too many think that length equals devotion; that is, the longer they pray the more God will listen to them (they are showing God their sincerity), and the more spiritual they will become.

God does not hear a person's prayer because it is long, but because his heart is genuinely poured out to God. Length has nothing to do with devotion, but a sincere heart does.

Long prayers are not forbidden. What is forbidden is the idea that long prayers are automatically heard by God. Christ prayed all night (Lu.6:12). The early disciples prayed and fasted, and sought God for ten days and nights waiting for the coming of the Holy Spirit (Ac.2:1f). A believer should sense the needs of the world so much that he is driven to seek God and His intervention for long periods of time, and the seeking should be often (Ep. 6:18).

Why do some pray long prayers?
a. Some feel long prayers convince God. They feel God has to be moved, nudged, and stirred to hear and answer.
b. Some feel they need long prayers to explain the situation. They feel God needs to be informed and made to understand a particular situation and how it has affected them.
c. Some feel long prayers make them more spiritual, more mature, and more devoted.
d. Some feel long prayers are just demanded of believers. It is expected; it is the religious and godly thing to do.
e. Some feel long prayers show God their sincerity. They secure God's approval by long prayers.
f. Some feel long prayers impress people. They show people just how deeply spiritual they really are.

What are ways to prevent the sins that arise from long prayers?

"Be not rash with thy mouth, and let not thine heart be hasty to utter anything before God: for God is in heaven, and thou upon earth: therefore let thy words be few" (Ec.5:2).

1. "Be not rash with thy mouth." Control your mouth. Do not let your mouth rattle on and on without thought. It will often rush and hurry with every thought that crosses your mind.
2. Be not "hasty to utter anything before God": sit still, be quiet, without saying a word for awhile. Do not rush forward to speak.
3. Think about who God is. Picture a man: his mouth is quiet; he has been still for some time. He has been preparing, gaining control of his mind and thoughts so he can appear before the Sovereign Majesty of the universe. He focuses his

thoughts upon God, the One who is in heaven far above the earth. He meditates upon God's sovereignty and majesty. God is the center of his thoughts (Ps.46:10).

4. "Let thy words be few." Speak—but make your words deliberate—just as deliberate as the words of any interviewer before a sovereign ruler. Request—just as any obedient son would request of a revered father. The person who approaches God like this speaks with respect and thought, with care and love. He speaks few words and straight to the point—all from a prepared heart and mind.

When should the believer spend a long time in prayer? There *are* special times when an extended prayer time is necessary. Some of the times are clearly seen in Scripture.

1. Sometimes a special pull to praise and adore God is felt within. When the believer feels this pull, he should get alone, spending a long time praising and worshipping God (see Ac.16:25).

2. Sometimes a special need arises. This may be the believer's own need or a friend's need. He should intercede until God gives the assurance that the need will be met (Ep.6:18; see Ac.12:1-5, esp. v.5).

3. Sometimes an unusual experience or event has taken place or is about to take place in the believer's life or ministry. He should get alone and share the event with God. And he should stay before God until the experience has taken place (courage, confidence, power, faith, love). (See Introduction—Mt.4:1-11.)

4. Sometimes a great trial or temptation is faced. A long session of prayer may be needed to gain strength and to keep the believer away from the trial or temptation. (See DEEPER STUDY # 1—Mt.4:1-11.)

5. Sometimes a matter needs to be worked through or a major decision needs to be made. Help and direction should be sought from God. God should be acknowledged in all of the believer's ways. He should remain before God until the answer is given. (See Ac.13:1-3, esp. 2.)

> **Thought 1.** Prayer is a matter of the heart, not a matter of words and length. Praying is sharing; it is sharing with God just like a person shares with any other person. Just as he shares thoughts, feelings, praise, and requests with others, so he shares with God.

> **Thought 2.** Prayer is a personal relationship. Prayer is not speaking into thin air. God may be *in secret* (v.6); He may be invisible, but He is there. He is there more than any other person who may be in our presence. He is the One whom all men are to know and to whom all men are to be vitally related. Too often, the awareness and consciousness of His presence are allowed to fade, and we just go through our long prayer with a wandering mind leaping from thought to thought. Long prayers lend themselves to this danger. How insincere! How irreverent! How often the heart of God must be cut and hurt!

> **Thought 3.** There are prayers of believers and prayers of the heathen. A distinction is made by Christ Himself. He says that both pray.
> (1) The heathen pray using vain repetition and speaking empty words.
> (2) The believer is vitally related to God; therefore, he prays to God who is his Father. He prays to God just as a son shares with his revered father.

> > **"But when ye pray, use not vain repetitions, as the heathen do: for they think that they shall be heard for their much speaking" (Mt.6:7).**
> > **"Woe unto you, scribes and Pharisees, hypocrites! for ye devour widows' houses, and for a pretence make long prayer: therefore ye shall receive the greater damnation" (Mt.23:14).**
> > **"All the labor of man is for his mouth, and yet the appetite is not filled" (Ec.6:7).**

3 (6:8) **Prayer:** the third great rule of prayer is forceful—trust God.

a. God knows the believer's need even before the believer asks. Why then should the believer pray?

Prayer demonstrates our need for God and our dependence upon God. Prayer gives time for concentrated sharing and communion between the believer and God. It is not enough for man to carry a knowledge of God in his mind as he walks through life. Man needs to have times when he is in the presence of God and can concentrate his thoughts and fellowship upon God. He needs such time with God just as he needs such time with his family and friends. Man is not meant to live in isolation from people nor from God. He must have times when he is in the presence of both man and God and can concentrate his thoughts and attention upon both.

The believer, therefore, does not pray only to have his needs met but to share and fellowship and to enrich his life with God.

> **Thought 1.** God knows the believer's needs. The believer does not have to worry about God's knowing or meeting his needs. The believer's concern should be living in the presence of God, taking enough time to share and to fellowship with God. The more he shares and fellowships with God, the more he will know God and learn to trust and to depend upon God's care and promises.

> **Thought 2.** God is the believer's Father. The believer is God's son. The believer can, therefore, *rest* in God and His promises. He does not have to strain and pray long in order for his Father to hear him. His Father already knows and cares. He is to get with His Father for long periods of time sharing and fellowshipping, learning and getting to know his Father intimately.

b. God desires to hear. God knows the believer's need even before the believer asks (see 2 Chr.16:9; Is.65:24). God desires to hear and answer the believer's prayer, to meet the believer's needs. God desires to work for the believer's deliverance and salvation (see outline and notes—Ro.8:23-27; 8:28-39. This is one of the great passages on assurance and confidence.)

c. God has ordained prayer as the medium through which He blesses and moves among men. (See DEEPER STUDY #3, *Prayer*—Mt.6:5-6; pt.2—1 Th.5:15-22).

> "Oh how great is thy goodness, which thou hast laid up for them that fear thee; which thou hast wrought for them that trust in thee before the sons of men!" (Ps.31:19).
> "Many sorrows shall be to the wicked: but he that trusteth in the Lord, mercy shall compass him about" (Ps.32:10).
> "The Lord redeemeth the soul of his servants: and none of them that trust in him shall be desolate" (Ps.34:22).
> "They that trust in the Lord shall be as mount Zion, which cannot be removed, but abideth for ever" (Ps.125:1).
> "Trust in the Lord with all thine heart; and lean not unto thine own understanding. In all thy ways acknowledge him, and he shall direct thy paths" (Pr.3:5-6).
> "The fear of man bringeth a snare: but whoso putteth his trust in the Lord shall be safe" (Pr.29:25).
> "Thou wilt keep him in perfect peace, whose mind is stayed on thee: because he trusteth in thee. Trust ye in the Lord for ever: for in the Lord JEHOVAH is everlasting strength" (Is.26:3-4).
> "Blessed is the man that trusteth in the LORD, and whose hope the LORD is. For he shall be as a tree planted by the waters, and that spreadeth out her roots by the river, and shall not see when heat cometh, but her leaf shall be green" (Je.17:7-8).

	N. The Model Prayer,[DS1] 6:9-13 *(Lu 11:2-4)*	in heaven. 11 Give us this day our daily bread.	b. For God's will[DS6] c. For daily bread[DS7]
1. There is surrender a. To our Father[DS2] in heaven[DS3] b. To God's Holy Name[DS4] **2. There is a request & plea** a. For God's kingdom[DS5]	9 After this manner therefore pray ye: Our Father which art in heaven, Hallowed be thy name. 10 Thy kingdom come. Thy will be done in earth, as *it is*	12 And forgive us our debts, as we forgive our debtors. 13 And lead us not into temptation, but deliver us from evil: For thine is the kingdom, and the power, and the glory, for ever. Amen.	d. For forgiveness[DS8] e. For deliverance[DS9] **3. There is praise** **4. There is commitment: Amen–"So be it"[DS10]**

DIVISION IV

THE TEACHINGS OF THE MESSIAH TO HIS DISCIPLES: THE GREAT SERMON ON THE MOUNT, 5:1–7:29

N. The Model Prayer (Part III), 6:9-13

(6:9-13) **Introduction—Prayer—Lord's Prayer**: What is the Lord's prayer? Is it a prayer to be recited as it so often is—just by memory, or just as a form prayer?

Note the words "After this manner...pray ye." Note also Luke's account where the disciples asked Jesus to teach them to pray (Lu.11:1-2). The prayer was given to show the disciples *how to pray*—how they should go about praying, not the *words* they should pray. The very context of what Christ had just taught shows this clearly (see Mt.6:5-8).

The Lord's prayer is a model prayer that is to be *prayed through*. It is "after this manner," *in this way*, *like this*, that a person is to pray. Christ was teaching the disciples how to pray. He was giving words, phrases, thoughts that are to be the points of the believer's prayer. The believer is to develop the points as he prays. An example would be something like this:

⇒ "Our Father...": "Thank you, Father, that you are our Father—that you have adopted us as children of God, sons and daughters of yours. Thank you for the believers of the world who make up the family of God. Thank you for the church, the body of Christ that gives us the family of God. Thank you for loving us that much." And on and on the believer is to pray.

⇒ "...which art in heaven": "Thank you for heaven—that you are in heaven—that you have chosen us to be with you in heaven. Thank you, Father, for the hope and anticipation of heaven." And on and on the believer prays.

Christ taught His disciples to pray *after this manner*. When the believer prays through the Lord's prayer, he finds he has covered the scope of what God wants him to pray. How much pain the Lord's heart must bear because of the way man has abused and misused His prayer! How desperately believers need to pray through the Lord's prayer! How desperately the *prophets and teachers* of the world need to pray as Christ taught! How much you and all of us as ministers of God need to preach and teach that the Lord's prayer is to be *prayed through* and not just recited.

1. There is surrender (v.9).
2. There is request and plea (vv.10-13).
3. There is praise (v.13).
4. There is commitment: Amen–"So be it" (v.13).

DEEPER STUDY # 1

(6:9-13) **Prayer**: What is prayer?

1. Prayer is sharing and fellowshipping with God (Mt.6:9). It is not enough for a person to have a knowledge of God as he walks through life. He needs to have times when he can get alone with God to concentrate his thoughts and attention upon God. He needs such times with God just as he needs such times with his family and friends. Man was not made to live in isolation from people nor from God. He must have times when he is in the presence of both man and God and can concentrate his thoughts and attention upon both (see note—Mt.6:8).

2. Prayer is surrendering to God (Mt.6:9). The believer surrenders himself and his time to God. There is no such thing as prayer without a person and time. A person must submit himself to God before he wills to pray, and even then he must take the time to pray. A person who has surrendered himself to God and is surrendering or taking his time to talk with God is praying (see note 1—Mt.6:9).

3. Prayer is requesting and pleading with God (Mt.6:10). It is demonstrating one's need and dependence upon God. It is pouring out one's heart in need and trusting God to meet one's need.

4. Prayer is acknowledging and praising God (Mt.6:9-10, 13). It is acknowledging God as the Sovereign and Majestic Lord to whom belongs the kingdom, the power, and the glory, forever.

---

1 (6:9) **Prayer—Surrender**: the believer's prayer is to be a surrender.

a. There is the surrender of the believer to God and to God's family.
   1) When a person genuinely says "Father," he is surrendering to God. He is...
   • denying humanism, self-sufficiency, and all other gods.
   • surrendering himself to the Father of the Lord Jesus Christ.
   • acknowledging the Father of the Lord Jesus Christ to be his own Father.

2) When a person prays "*our* Father," a person is surrendering his independency and accepting God's family. He is assuming his responsibility in the family of God.

b. There is the surrender of the believer to *heaven*, the spiritual world or dimension of being. The believer surrenders and sets his mind and heart upon the Kingdom of God and His righteousness. His whole being is surrendered and committed to seeking the things of the spiritual world. (See outline and notes—Ep.1:3.)

c. There is the surrender of the believer to the holy name of God. The believer just bows in total and abject poverty, in nothingness before the holy name of God. He is swallowed up in the knowledge of the "hallowedness," the sovereignty and majesty of God's being. God is all and man is nothing! He is totally dependent upon God.

Note: when a person reaches this point of surrender, then he is ready to present his needs to God. He is ever so conscious that only God can meet his needs.

DEEPER STUDY # 2

(6:9) **God—Father**: God is addressed as "Our Father." Father denotes a family relationship and shows three things.

1. It shows that "God [who is]...in heaven" is the believer's Father. Thus, a relationship with the unseen heavenly world and the seen earthly world is established. God represents the unseen world and the believer represents the seen world. In the believer, a whole new being is created (a new creature) and a whole new world is recognized and established: a world of the spirit and the physical, of the unseen and the seen, of heaven and earth (2 Co.5:17; Ep.4:23-24; Col.4:10. Especially see notes—Ep.2:11-18; pt.4—2:14-15; 4:17.)

2. The word *Father* establishes a relationship between a believer and all other believers. All believers belong to the same family; they all have common interests, cares, and responsibilities within the family.

3. The word *Father* pinpoints God as the believer's source. God, as Father, is the Person who loves and provides and cares for the believer's needs, even as an earthly father looks after his child (Mt.6:25-34, esp.33; Lu.11:11-13; Ps.103:13; Mal.3:17; see He.2:18; 4:15-16).

Thought 1. *Our Father* is the first point to pray. The believer is to pray *after this manner*.
⇒ Father, thank you *for yourself*: that you are *our Father*....
⇒ Thank you for adopting us as children of God: that you have chosen us....
⇒ Thank you for "the household of faith," for the "family of God"....

Thought 2. The phrase *Our Father* says three things about prayer.
(1) The believer is not to pray alone—not always. The word *our* shows this. Christ has just taught that a person should pray alone. He now says there are times when a person should pray with others. God is *our Father*.
(2) The believer is taught to whom to pray: to God and to Him alone.
(3) The believer is taught to address God as *Father*. He is taught what his relationship to God is to be, that of a child to a Father.

> **"If ye then, being evil, know how to give good gifts unto your children, how much more shall your Father which is in heaven give good things to them that ask him?" (Mt.7:11).**
> **"And if ye call on the Father, who without respect of persons judgeth according to every man's work, pass the time of your sojourning here in fear" (1 Pe.1:17).**

Thought 3. God is *our* Father. God has no favorites: "God is no respecter of persons" (Ac.10:34).
(1) God is *our Father* by creation; that is, He is the Father of all men everywhere because He is the Creator of all men (Ge.1:1; Mal.2:10; Is.64:8; Ac.27:28).
(2) God is *our Father* by re-creation (2 Co.5:17) and adoption (see DEEPER STUDY # 2—Ga.4:5-6; see Ep.1:5). He is "our Father" to all who believe in the Lord Jesus Christ and the redemption that is in Him (Ep.2:19).

> **"For ye have not receive the spirit of bondage again to fear; but ye have received the Spirit of adoption, whereby we cry, Abba, Father" (Ro.8:15).**
> **"But when the fulness of the time was come, God sent forth his Son, made of a woman, made under the law, to redeem them that were under the law, that we might receive the adoption of sons. And because ye are sons, God hath sent forth the Spirit of his Son into your hearts, crying, Abba, Father" (Ga.4:4-6).**

Thought 4. There is one time in particular when the believer must approach God as Father: when returning to God and repenting of sin (see the prodigal son, Lu.15:18).

Thought 5. *Our Father* settles all the relationships in the world.
(1) It settles a person's relationship with himself. Every person fails and comes short, and sometimes he gets down on himself. He feels like a failure—hopeless, helpless, worthless, useless. *Our Father* says that such a person matters; he always matters to God. He can come to the Father and share his concerns.
(2) It settles a person's relationship with others (see Thought 3).

DEEPER STUDY # 3

(6:9) **Heaven**: the word is plural in the Greek, heavens. The New Testament speaks of at least three heavens:
⇒ the atmosphere surrounding the earth (see Mt.6:26, "the fowls [birds] of the air").
⇒ the outer space of heavenly bodies (see Mt.24:29; Re.6:13).

⇒ the place above and beyond the physical dimension of being where God's presence is fully manifested. In modern language "the above and beyond" is another dimension of being entirely; it is *the spiritual world, another dimension of being*. It is a spiritual world where God's presence is fully manifested and where Christ and His followers live awaiting the glorious day of redemption. That glorious day of redemption is the day when God shall take the imperfect heavens and earth (the physical dimension) and transform them into the new heavens and earth (the spiritual and eternal dimension). (See note—2 Pe.3:8-10, esp. 3:11-14 for more discussion.)

Thought 1. "Our Father...in Heaven" is the second point to be prayed. The believer is to pray *after this manner*:
⇒ Father, thank you for heaven: the hope, the anticipation of heaven....
⇒ Thank you that you are in heaven....
⇒ Thank you for your promise that we shall be where you are.... (Jn.17:24).

Thought 2. Note several lessons.
(1) The believer must direct his prayers to heaven. God's throne is in heaven (Ps.103:19), and it is before the throne of God that Christ is appearing as the Advocate or Mediator for the believer.

> "But he, being full of the Holy Ghost, looked up stedfastly into heaven, and saw the glory of God, and Jesus standing on the right hand of God, and said, Behold, I see the heavens opened, and the Son of man standing on the right hand of God" (Ac.7:55-56).
> "For there is one God, and one mediator between God and men, the man Christ Jesus" (1 Ti.2:5).
> "Now of the things which we have spoken this is the sum: We have such an high priest, who is set on the right hand of the throne of the Majesty in the heavens" (He.8:1).
> "But now hath he obtained a more excellent ministry, by how much also he is the mediator of a better covenant, which was established upon better promises" (He.8:6).
> "And for this cause he is the mediator of the new testament, that by means of death, for the redemption of the transgressions that were under the first testament, they which are called might receive the promise of eternal inheritance" (He.9:15).

(2) How should we approach God? The words "Our Father...in heaven" tell us.
   (a) *Father* says that we can approach Him boldly to "find grace to help in time of need" (He.4:16).
   (b) *In heaven* says that we are to approach respectfully, in reverence and fear and awe (Ps.111:9; see Ec.5:2).
(3) The heavens reveal the power and glory of God. Space shows His handiwork (Ps.19:1; 150:1). When connected together, the words *Our Father* and the words *in heaven* put two great things together: the love of God and the power of God. God through love has become *our Father*, and *God in heaven* has shown His glorious power which is at the disposal of His child. The believer's Father has the power to do anything, even to hang the world in space (Ep.3:20; Ps.121:1-8).
(4) The believer's true citizenship is *in heaven* (Ph.3:20). God is there; the Lord Jesus is also there (He.8:1; see Ps.103:19). Therefore, the longing of the mature believer's heart is to be in heaven where His Father and His Lord are. He directs his attention, prayers, energy, and life toward heaven.

> "Notwithstanding in this rejoice not, that the spirits are subject unto you; but rather rejoice, because your names are written in heaven" (Lu.10:20).
> "In my Father's house are many mansions: if it were not so, I would have told you. I go to prepare a place for you" (Jn.14:2).
> "For we know that if our earthly house of this tabernacle were dissolved, we have a building of God, an house not made with hands, eternal in the heavens" (2 Co.5:1).
> "For our conversation [citizenship] is in heaven; from whence also we look for the Saviour, the Lord Jesus Christ" (Ph.3:20).
> "For the hope which is laid up for you in heaven, whereof ye heard before in the word of the truth of the gospel" (Col.1:5).
> "For he [Abraham] looked for a city which hath foundations, whose builder and maker is God" (He.11:10).

(5) God sees all from heaven (Ps.33:13-19).
⇒ He sees all the sons of men.
⇒ He looks upon all the inhabitants of the earth.
⇒ He considers all their works.

However, there is one thing in particular that God sees: the person who fears Him and hopes in His mercy. He sees this person in order to deliver his soul from death (Ps.33:18-19). This is one of the prime reasons the believer keeps his eyes upon heaven.

DEEPER STUDY # 4
(6:9) **Hallowed be** (hagiastheto): to be counted holy; to be treated holy; to be counted and treated as different. The prayer is for men to count and treat the Name of God differently, to set His Name apart from all other names (see note—1 Pe.1:15-16).

Thought 1. "Hallowed be thy name" is the third point to be prayed. The believer is to pray *after this manner:*
⇒ Father, hallowed is your Name. Your Name is holy, set apart, different from all other names.
⇒ There is none but you...you and you alone. You are above, before, over all....

Thought 2. Note several lessons.
(1) God's Name is holy, righteous, pure. It is above, before, and over all names. Therefore, the believer's prayer is for God's Name to be adored and honored by all men. (See outline and notes—Mt.5:33-37 for a contrast in how some men treat the Name of God.)
(2) The first thing prayer should do is praise and glorify God. That is the point Christ is making in the words...
• "Our Father...
• which art in heaven...
• hallowed be thy Name."

God has done everything; He has made the world and given life to it. Man owes his very life to God. Therefore, the first thing man should do is praise God.

"Every good gift and every perfect gift is from above" (Js.1:17).

(3) The first purpose of man is to glorify God by his life: "Be ye holy; for I am holy" (1 Pe.1:15-16). Life includes speech; therefore, man should be praising God's holiness by word as well as by life. In fact, since the primary purpose of man is to be holy, then it follows that the first words spoken to God should be praising His holiness. All prayer should be centered around praising God for who He is—in all His holiness and fullness. His Name is *hallowed*, different, set apart form all other names. And thank God that His Name is set apart, for imagine what life would be if His Name should be no more than a man's name.

"If in this life only we have hope in Christ, we are of all men most miserable" (1 Co.15:19).

(4) God's glory is the very reason Christ came to earth (Jn.17:1-26, esp. vs.1, 4-6, 22-26). God says He shall be exalted in the earth even among the heathen (Ps.46:10; see Ps.2:1-5, esp. vs.4-5). How much man needs to fix his mind upon the holiness and glory of God's Name!

"For thus saith the high and lofty One that inhabiteth eternity, whose name is Holy; I dwell in the high and holy place, with him also that is of a contrite and humble spirit, to revive the spirit of the humble, and to revive the heart of the contrite ones" (Is.57:15).
"Daniel answered and said, Blessed be the name of God for ever and ever: for wisdom and might are his" (Da.2:20).
"Be still, and know that I am God: I will be exalted among the heathen, I will be exalted in the earth" (Ps.46:10).

(5) Men praise and honor each other among themselves. Men glorify men, even make idols of them (see note—Mt.6:2). Some are more loyal to the names of the famous (athletes, stars, politicians) than they are to the Name of God. They are more disturbed when the name of their idol is spoken of disrespectfully than they are when the name of God is cursed. How differently Scripture presents God's Name: "Hallowed be thy name." God says that the man who curses His Name is to be judged severely (Ex.20:7).

---

2 (6:10-13) **Prayer:** the believer is to request and plea for several things (see DEEPER STUDIES # 5-9—Mt.6:10, 6:11; 6:12; 6:13).

DEEPER STUDY # 5
(6:10) **Kingdom of God**: see DEEPER STUDY # 3—Mt.19:23-24.

Thought 1. "Thy kingdom come" is the first request to be prayed. The believer is to pray *after this manner*:
⇒ Father, let your kingdom come right here on this earth. Let Christ rule and reign in the hearts and the *lives* of all. Send Him, His kingdom, His sovereignty right now. God, I pray, even so come Lord Jesus, come...

Thought 2. The Kingdom of God is to be the focus of the believer's requests, the very first thing for which he asks. There are three reasons for this.
(1) It is the very message that Jesus Christ and the early apostles preached and taught and prayed (Mt.3:2; 4:17; 5:3, 10, 19-20).
(2) It is the very thing for which God longs. He longs for the day when He will rule and reign in the hearts of all men, perfectly—the day when all men will willingly submit and serve Him—the day when all thoughts, all words, all behavior will be exactly what they should be.
(3) It is the very substance of the believer's life, or at least it should be. The believer should be living and loving and having his being for God and God alone. His whole focus and attention, energy and effort should be centered on the rule and reign of God on earth.

"And saying, Repent ye: for the kingdom of heaven is at hand" (Mt.3:2).
"From that time Jesus began to preach, and to say, Repent: for the kingdom of heaven is at hand" (Mt.4:17).

"Blessed are the poor in spirit: for theirs is the kingdom of heaven" (Mt.5:3).

"Blessed are they which are persecuted for righteousness' sake: for theirs is the kingdom of heaven" (Mt.5:10).

"For the kingdom of God is not meat and drink; but righteousness, and peace, and joy in the Holy Ghost" (Ro.14:17).

Thought 3. "Thy kingdom come" is future. It is a request for something that is not now existing on earth. It is a request for the rule and reign of God and of His kingdom. The believer is to pray *thy kingdom come*.

"For I say unto you, That except your righteousness shall exceed the righteousness of the scribes and Pharisees, ye shall in no case enter into the kingdom of heaven" (Mt.5:20).

"Then shall the King say unto them on his right hand, Come, ye blessed of my Father, inherit the kingdom prepared for you from the foundation of the world" (Mt.25:34).

"Confirming the souls of the disciples, and exhorting them to continue in the faith, and that we must through much tribulation enter into the kingdom of God" (Ac.14:22).

"Hearken, my beloved brethren, Hath not God chosen the poor of this world rich in faith, and heirs of the kingdom which he hath promised to them that love him?" (Js.2:5).

"Even so, come Lord Jesus, come" (Re.22:20).

Thought 4. God's kingdom *is* available. God's kingdom is desperately needed on earth right now. So much just eats and gnaws away at man—so much rebellion, wickedness, evil, enmity, bitterness, hatred, murder, injustice, deprivation, and hunger. God's rule and reign are needed now. The believer needs to see the urgency to pray and to pray consistently "Thy kingdom come," and to live as if God's kingdom had already come.

DEEPER STUDY # 6

(6:10) **God, Will of:** "Thy will be done" says three critical things to God.

1. That we will work to please God in all we do. We will do our part to see that God's will is done on earth.

2. That God can do with us as He pleases. No matter what He chooses for us, we put ourselves at His disposal, for His use—even if it requires the sacrifice of all we are and have.

3. That we will not be displeased with what God does. We may not understand; it may not make sense; there may be question after question; but we know that God's will is best, and He will work all things out for good.

Thought 1. "Thy will be done in earth, as it is in heaven" is the second request to be prayed. The believer is to pray *after this manner*:

⇒ Father, your will be done: your will and your will alone. There is no will but your will. Let it be done right here on earth....

Thought 2. There are four wills that struggle for man's obedience.

(1) Man's own will (Ro.12:1-2; see Ro.7:15f; Ga.5:17).

(2) Other men's wills (1 Pe.4:2).

(3) Satan's will (Jn.8:44).

(4) God's will (Ep.5:15-17, esp. vs.17; Ph.2:13; 1 Jn.2:17).

Thought 3. Note three significant lessons.

(1) Many call God King, but they do not honor Him as a King. They do not do His will. Their profession is false, and tragically it creates an image of a false and meaningless King to the world.

(2) We *must know God's will* if God's will is to be done. This requires study: "Study to show thyself approved unto God" (2 Ti.2:15). The only way God's will can be done is for us to study His Word and ask for the wisdom and strength to apply it to our lives (2 Ti.3:16).

(3) We are to ask for God's will to be done *on earth*. The earth is the place where God's will is so desperately needed. It is the place...

• where there is so much sin and corruption
• where there is so much suffering and pain
• where there is so much struggling and death
• where the believer faces his trials

"And Mary said, Behold the handmaid of the Lord; be it unto me according to thy word. And the angel departed from her" (Lu.1:38).

"Neither yield ye your members as instruments of unrighteousness unto sin: but yield yourselves unto God, as those that are alive from the dead, and your members as instruments of righteousness unto God" (Ro.6:13).

"Submit yourselves therefore to God. Resist the devil, and he will flee from you" (Js.4:7).

"I delight to do thy will, O my God: yea, thy law is within my heart" (Ps.40:8).

"Teach me to do thy will; for thou art my God: thy spirit is good; lead me into the land of uprightness" (Ps.143:10).

(4) "Thy will be done in earth as it is in heaven." The believer is praying for *heaven (heaven's rule) to come to earth*. He is making a commitment to make earth more like heaven.
- By yielding himself "to God, as those that are alive from the dead...." (Ro.6:13).
- By going and teaching "all nations...teaching them all things whatsoever I [Christ] have commanded you" (Mt.28:19-20).

DEEPER STUDY # 7

(6:11) **Bread**: bread is the basic necessity of life, the symbol of all that is necessary for survival and for a full life. There is much meaning in this simple request.

1. "Give *us...our* bread." The words *our* and *us* overcome selfishness and show concern for others. Any person who goes to bed hungry should be of concern to the believer.

2. "*This day*." This eliminates worry and anxiety about tomorrow and the distant future. It also teaches and helps us to trust God day by day. "The just shall live by faith...." day by day.

3. "Our *daily* bread." Every believer has a portion of daily bread which is his. He does not ask for someone else's bread but for his own. He seeks and works for his own bread; he does not think of stealing or of eating from another man's table (2 Th.3:10).

4. "Give us...*bread*." We ask for the necessities, not the desserts of this world.

5. "*Give us*...bread." The believer confesses his inadequacy and dependency upon God. He is dependent upon God even for the basics of life.

6. "Give...this day our *daily bread*." This teaches the believer to come to God daily in prayer and trust Him to meet his needs.

Thought 1. "Give us this day our daily bread" is the third request to be prayed. The believer should pray *after this manner*:
⇒ Father give us our bread this day, spiritually as well as physically. Feed our souls and our bodies.
⇒ Make this a glorious day in You. And, O God, the world is starving for You, and many are starving from hunger....

Thought 2. God cares for man and his welfare.
(1) He cares for man's physical well-being (Mt.6:11; Mt.6:25-34).

   "Therefore take no thought, saying, What shall we eat? or, What shall we drink? or, Wherewithal shall we be clothed? (For after all these things do the Gentiles seek:) for your heavenly Father knoweth that ye have need of all these things. But seek ye first the kingdom of God, and his righteousness; and all these things shall be added unto you" (Mt.6:31-33).

(2) He cares for man's mental and emotional well-being.

   "For God hath not given us the spirit of fear; but of power, and of love, and of a sound mind" (2 Ti.1:7).
   "Finally, brethren, whatsoever things are true, whatsoever things are honest, whatsoever things are just, whatsoever things are pure, whatsoever things are lovely, whatsoever things are of good report; if there be any virtue, and if there be any praise, think on these things" (Ph.4:8).
   "But the God of all grace, who hath called us unto his eternal glory by Christ Jesus, after that ye have suffered a while, make you perfect, stablish, strengthen, settle you" (1 Pe.5:10).

(3) He cares for man's spiritual well-being.

   "Know ye not that ye are the temple of God, and that the Spirit of God dwelleth in you? If any man defile the temple of God, him shall God destroy; for the temple of God is holy, which temple ye are" (1 Co.3:16-17).
   "What? know ye not that your body is the temple of the Holy Ghost which is in you, which ye have of God, and ye are not your own? For ye are bought with a price: therefore glorify God in your body, and in your spirit, which are God's" (1 Co.6:19-20).

Thought 3. God cares for the human body. Several things show this.
(1) He said to ask for the necessities of life, daily (Mt.6:11).
(2) He sent His only Son into the world in a human body.
(3) He raised up Christ in His body, a resurrected body.
(4) He promises to give a new resurrected body to the believer. The believer will dwell in *the resurrected body* forever.
(5) He has chosen the believer's body to be "the temple of the Holy Spirit" (1 Co.6:19-20).

Thought 4. This simple request is a great lesson for both the rich and the poor.
(1) The rich man feels self-sufficient, as though what he possesses came from his own hands. Therefore, he thinks, "Who is the Lord?"

(2) The poor man has nothing and is often forced to steal. Thus, he raises his fist in anger and curses God for his state of life.

> "Give me neither poverty nor riches; feed me with food convenient [that I need] for me: lest I be full, and deny thee, and say, Who is the Lord? or lest I be poor, and steal, and take the name of my God in vain" (Pr.30:8-9).

The believer is to trust God for the necessities of life and praise God for what he receives. He has learned, "In whatsoever state I am, therewith to be content" (Ph.4:11; see 4:12-13).

DEEPER STUDY # 8

(6:12) **Forgiveness, Spiritual**: the word *debts* (opheilema) means dues, duties, that which is owed, that which is legally due. In relation to sin, it means a failure to pay one's debts, one's dues; a failure to do one's duty; to keep one's responsibilities.

God has given man certain responsibilities, certain things to do and not to do. Every man has failed at some point to do what he should. Certainly no man would ever claim he has fulfilled his duty perfectly—without any failure, without any shortcoming. Sin is universal. Everyone fails in his duty at some point to some degree. Everyone needs to pray "forgive us our debts, as we forgive our debtors."

This prayer is asking God to do three things.

1. To forgive *the debt of sin*. One has failed God in his duty; therefore, he needs God to forgive his debt.

2. To forgive *the debt of guilt or punishment*. One who has failed to pay his debts is guilty; therefore, he is to pay the consequences; he is to be punished. This is the reason he must pray "Father, forgive my debts...."

3. To forgive *his debts just as he has forgiven* his debtors. This is asking God to forgive one exactly as he forgives others. If one forgives, God forgives. If one does not forgive, God does not forgive. Therefore, any person who holds anything against another person is not forgiven his sins, no matter what he may think or has been told by another person. (See Mt.6:14-15).

Thought 1. "Forgive us our debts, as we forgive our debtors" is the fourth request to be prayed. The believer should pray *after this manner*.

(1) Father, forgive me—have mercy upon me, the sinner, the nothing. O' God, You are all—have mercy....

(2) Father, forgive others—all others. I hold nothing within. O' God, if there is anything within my heart against anyone, help me to forgive....

Thought 2. In seeking forgiveness we have a duty both to God and to man.

(1) Our duty to God is to ask forgiveness when we fail to do His will.

> "If we confess our sins, he is faithful and just to forgive us our sins, and to cleanse us from all unrighteousness" (1 Jn.1:9).
> "Let the wicked forsake his way, and the unrighteous man his thoughts: and let him return unto the LORD, and he will have mercy upon him; and to our God, for he will abundantly pardon" (Is.55:7).
> "And I will cleanse them from all their iniquity, whereby they have sinned against me; and I will pardon all their iniquities, whereby they have sinned, and whereby they have transgressed against me" (Je.33:8).

(2) Our duty to man is to forgive his sins against us.

> "And when ye stand praying, forgive, if ye have ought against any: that your Father also which is in heaven may forgive you your trespasses" (Mk.11:25).
> "And if he trespass against thee seven times in a day, and seven times in a day turn again to thee, saying, I repent; thou shalt forgive him" (Lu.17:4).
> "And be ye kind one to another, tenderhearted, forgiving one another, even as God for Christ's sake hath forgiven you" (Ep.4:32).
> "Forbearing one another, and forgiving one another, if any man have a quarrel against any: even as Christ forgave you, so also do ye" (Col.3:13).

> If we wish to be forgiven ourselves, both duties have to be performed. We must forgive those who sin against us (Mt.6:12), and we must ask forgiveness for our sins (1 Jn.1:9).

Thought 3. There are those who do us much evil. In this world, many say and do all manner of evil against us. Bad news and evil purposes run wild, and it is not always *outside* the church, nor *outside* the family. Sometimes terrible evil is committed by word and act both within the church and within a person's family (Ep.4:30-32; see Mt.10:21; Mk.13:12-13). Christ says we must not react nor be harsh toward those who sin severely against us, but we must forgive. We must forgive if we wish to be forgiven.

⇒ Some smite us (Mt.5:39). ⇒ Some sue us (Mt.5:40).
⇒ Some despitefully use us (Mt.5:44). ⇒ Some curse us (Mt.5:44)
⇒ Some hate us (Mt.5:44). ⇒ Some persecute us (Mt.5:44)
⇒ Some compel us against our will (Mt.5:41). ⇒ Some spread rumors about us (Mt.5:11).

Thought 4. There are four things a believer must do when sinned against.
(1) The believer must understand (Pr.11:12; 15:21; 17:27-28; see Ep.1:8). There is always a reason why a person sins against a believer. Too often we forget this.
   (a) A person may be mistreated by someone who is close to him. He may be withdrawn from, neglected, and ignored. Therefore, he may react against a believer, and the reaction may range from self-pity to bitterness and hostility.
   (b) A person may be tired, aggravated, and worried. Therefore, he may become too direct or cutting or harsh toward the believer.
   (c) A person may be of a shy nature or sense inferiority; therefore, he may act unfriendly and unconcerned toward the believer.
   (d) A person may have rumor and gossip and wild imaginations shared with him, especially by a person who has been hurt; he may be lied to and misinformed. Therefore, he may act suspicious and have nothing to do with the believer.
   (e) A person may have a great need for attention and for emotional support. Therefore, the person may imagine, exaggerate, blame, or accuse a believer in order to rally the support of friends and to gain the attention needed.
(2) The believer must forbear (Ep.4:2; Col.3:13).
(3) The believer must forgive (Ep.4:31-32).
(4) The believer must forget, that is, not harbor the wrong done to him (Ph.3:13; see 2 Co.10:5).

Thought 5. Note four additional lessons that need to be noted.
(1) An unforgiving spirit causes pain and hurt and tragedy—both to oneself and others. It can ruin lives, especially the lives of those closest and dearest to oneself.
(2) We can curse ourselves by praying the Lord's prayer. We are in trouble when praying the Lord's prayer if we are angry and do not forgive those who sin against us: "Father...forgive us...*as we forgive* our debtors." We pronounce the very same judgment upon ourselves that we hold for others.
(3) Forgiveness is conditional. The reason is simply explained. We have sinned against God, and others have sinned against us. If we want God to forgive us, we must forgive those who have sinned against us. How can we expect God to forgive us if we do not forgive those who have sinned against us? We can expect no better treatment than we give.
(4) Forgiving others is evidence that God has forgiven our sins.

DEEPER STUDY # 9
(6:13) **Temptation—Deliverance**: God does not lead a man to sin; He tempts no man (Js.1:13). What Christ is saying is two things.
   1. Pray—pray that God will keep you from the awful pull of temptation. The believer is to have a sense of his personal weakness against temptation.
   2. Pray—pray that God will deliver you from evil. The Greek says "from the evil one," that is, Satan. The request is for God to rescue, preserve, and guard us. He, the evil one, is so deceptive and powerful; he is as powerful as a roaring lion (1 Pe.5:8).
   The plea and the cry is for God to deliver us from (1) temptation and (2) from the evil one. (See Ro.8:31; 1 Jn.4:4; see 1 Co.10:13. Also see outlines—Js.4:7-10; see note 1 and DEEPER STUDY # 1—Lu.4:1-2.)

Thought 1. "Lead us not into temptation, but deliver us from the evil one" is the fifth request to be prayed. The believer should pray "after this manner":
   ⇒ "Father, lead us not into temptation. Temptation comes so often; its pull is so strong. We get in the way so much. We seek our own way and react at every turn. O' God do not leave us to ourselves....
   ⇒ "And, dear Father, deliver us from the evil one. He is the master of deceit and paints such a beautiful picture. If you leave us to ourselves, we will fall. And, O' God, he is capable of being 'a roaring lion' seeking to devour us. Deliver us—rescue us—preserve us—guard us...."

Thought 2. Once we have been forgiven our sins (v.12), we must ask God to keep us from sinning again. Two things are essential to keep us from sin: (1) deliverance from temptation (see DEEPER STUDY # 1—Lu.4:1-2) and (2) deliverance from *the evil one* (see DEEPER STUDY # 1—Re.12:9).

Thought 3. This request is a necessity for every believer. Why? There are two reasons.
(1) All believers are tempted and tempted often, not by strange things, but by things that are common to all. Temptations do come and will come to all—the same temptations (1 Co.10:13.)
(2) No believer stands above falling:

"Wherefore let him that thinketh he standeth take heed lest he fall." (1 Co.10:12).

Thought 4. Temptation is to be prayed against for two reasons.
(1) Because sin causes God great hurt and pain (Ps.15:4).
(2) Because sin causes great trouble, guilt, and grief for both oneself and others (Lu.19:41-44; see Mt.23:37; Lu.13:34).

Thought 5. The believer must have help in overcoming *the evil one*. The *evil one* attacks (1) by deception (2 Co.11:3, 14-15; Re.12:9) and (2) by direct assault, seeking to devour (1 Pe.5:8).

Thought 6. In dealing with *the evil one,* the believer needs to remember two things.
(1) "Greater is He that is in you, than he that is in the world" (1 Jn.4:4).
(2) "If God be for us, who can be against us?" (Ro.8:31; see Ro.8:31-39).

> "There hath no temptation taken you but such as is common to man: but God is faithful, who will not suffer you to be tempted above that ye are able; but will with the temptation also make a way to escape, that ye may be able to bear it" (1 Co.10:13).
> "My brethren, count it all joy when ye fall into divers temptations; knowing this, that the trying of your faith worketh patience" (Js.1:2-3).
> "Blessed is the man that endureth temptation: for when he is tried, he shall receive the crown of life, which the Lord hath promised to them that love him" (Js.1:12).
> "The Lord knoweth how to deliver the godly out of temptations, and to reserve the unjust unto the day of judgment to be punished" (2 Pe.2:9).
> "Now unto him that is able to keep you from falling, and to present you faultless before the presence of his glory with exceeding joy, to the only wise God our Saviour, be glory and majesty, dominion and power, both now and ever" (Jude 24-25).
> "Because thou hast kept the word of my patience, I also will keep thee from the hour of temptation, which shall come upon all the world, to try them that dwell upon the earth" (Re.3:10).

3 (6:13) **Doxology—The kingdom and the power and the glory**: there is praise and commitment. These words are not in the best and oldest manuscripts of the Greek. Many scholars believe the doxology was added at a later date to be used in public worship. However, there is a similar doxology by David (1 Chr.29:11). The point of the doxology is to stress that everything belongs to God.
a. He is *the Source* of the kingdom and the power and the glory.
b. He is *the Possessor* of the kingdom and the power and the glory.
c. He is *the Recipient* of the kingdom and the power and the glory.

The believer belongs to the kingdom and the power and the glory of God.
1. The believer belongs to God's kingdom: God has accepted the believer into the Kingdom of God and promises to transport him into the kingdom and its glory either at death or at the Lord's return.
2. The believer belongs to God's power: God has delivered him from sin and death and continues to deliver him daily.
3. The believer belongs to God's glory: God has done all for the believer that "in the ages to come He [God] might show the exceeding riches of His grace in His kindness toward us through Christ Jesus" (Ep.2:7).

Thought 1. "Thine is the kingdom, and the power, and the glory, forever. Amen" is the third major point to pray.
(1) Father, yours is the kingdom, the right to rule and reign....
(2) Yours is the power, the only power that can really rule and govern....
(3) Yours is the glory. O' God, all glory belongs to you....

Thought 2. Note three significant points.
(1) "Thine is the kingdom" says two things.
  (a) The right to rule and reign throughout the universe is God's. The only perfect and eternal government is God's. The only government that possesses utopia, the very best of all, and that lasts forever is God's.
  (b) The right to rule and reign belongs to no one else but God. Only God's government can bring utopia: love, joy, peace, and the very best of life.

> "God that made the world and all things therein, seeing that he is Lord of heaven and earth, dwelleth not in temples made with hands; neither is worshipped with men's hands, as though he needed any thing, seeing he giveth to all life, and breath, and all things" (Ac.17:24-25).
> "Know therefore this day, and consider it in thine heart, that the LORD he is God in heaven above, and upon the earth beneath: there is none else" (De.4:39).
> "Both riches and honor come of thee, and thou reignest over all; and in thine hand is power and might; and in thine hand it is to make great, and to give strength unto all" (1 Chr.29:12).
> "That men may know that thou, whose name alone is JEHOVAH, art the most high over all the earth" (Ps.83:18).
> "The LORD reigneth, he is clothed with majesty; the LORD is clothed with strength, wherewith he hath girded himself: the world also is stablished, that it cannot be moved" (Ps.93:1).
> "Daniel answered and said, Blessed be the name of God for ever and ever: for wisdom and might are his: and he changeth the times and the seasons: he removeth kings, and setteth up kings: he giveth wisdom unto the wise, and knowledge to them that know understanding" (Da.2:20-21).
> "And all the inhabitants of the earth are reputed as nothing: and he doeth according to his will in the army of heaven, and none can stay his hand, or say unto him, What doest thou?" (Da.4:35).

(2) "Thine is the power" says two things.
    (a) God alone has the power to create and sustain perfect government. He alone has the power to support and bring perfect government to man and his earth.
    (b) God alone has the power to change men so that they can escape death and live forever within a perfect government. He alone has the power to stir men to live in love, joy, and peace and to serve completely and unselfishly so that all may have the very best.
(3) "Thine is the glory" says that God alone deserves all the honor and praise and glory. For what? For all. He is all in all.

Thought 3. The one subject that is to dominate prayer is *praising God*. The fact that the Lord's prayer begins with praise (surrender, v.9) and ends with praise (v.13ᵇ) shows this.
⇒ God *does not need* praise. He has the praise of multitudes of angels, but He *deserves* our praise.
⇒ God created us with the ability to praise Him. He must *want* our praise.
⇒ A genuine believer is always praising God's Name before all.

DEEPER STUDY # 10
(6:13) **Amen**: so be it; it is and shall be so. When spoken by God, *Amen* means it is and shall be so, unequivocally. When spoken by man it is a petition meaning, *Let it be*. Here, in the Lord's Prayer, the word *Amen* is a word of commitment. When a man prays the Lord's prayer and closes by saying *Amen* (let it be), he is committing himself to do his part for the things which have been prayed.

	O. The Basic Principle of Prayer: Forgiveness,^{DS1,2} 6:14-15 (Mk 11:25-26)
1. The promise: Forgive others & be forgiven	14 For if ye forgive men their trespasses, your heavenly Father will also forgive you:
2. The warning: Refuse to forgive others & be unforgiven	15 But if ye forgive not men their trespasses, neither will your Father forgive your trespasses.

DIVISION IV

THE TEACHINGS OF THE MESSIAH TO HIS DISCIPLES: THE GREAT SERMON ON THE MOUNT, 5:1–7:29

O. The Basic Principle of Prayer: Forgiveness, 6:14-15

(6:14-15) **Introduction—Forgiveness**: note the first word, "for." This connects these verses to the Lord's Prayer. Immediately after closing the Lord's Prayer, Jesus explained why He had said that forgiveness is conditional (Mt.6:12). This was a necessary explanation for two reasons.

1. The very idea that a person must forgive others in order for God to forgive him was totally new. It was a shocking concept, an eye-opener. It had to be explained.

2. The very idea of forgiveness is just what it says: it is forgiving. God knows that He cannot forgive an unforgiving heart. His nature of love and justice will not permit Him to indulge in sin and give license to the passions of a man's unforgiving spirit. He can forgive only where the mercy and tenderness of forgiveness are found. Therefore, Christ had to teach the basic principle of prayer—forgiveness (Mt.18:21-35; Mk.11:25-26; Lu.6:37; 17:3-4; Ep.4:32). (See DEEPER STUDY #4—Mt.26:28.)

1. The promise: forgive others and be forgiven (v.14).
2. The warning: refuse to forgive others and be unforgiven (v.15).

DEEPER STUDY # 1
(6:14-15) **Forgiveness**: there are several prerequisites to forgiveness. For a man to be forgiven, he must do several things.

1. He must confess his sins (1 Jn.1:9; see 1 Jn.1:8-10).
2. He must have faith in God: a belief that God will actually forgive (He.11:6).
3. He must repent (turn away from and forsake his sins) and turn to God in a renewed commitment (see note—Acts 3:19; note 7 and DEEPER STUDY #1—17:29-30; note—Lu.17:3-4).
4. He must forgive those who have wronged him (Mt.6:14-15). Hard feelings or anger against a person is sin. It is evidence that a person has not truly turned from his sins and that he is *not really* sincere in seeking forgiveness.

DEEPER STUDY # 2
(6:14-15) **Forgiveness**: there are four different attitudes toward forgiveness.

1. The attitude of the agnostic or doubter. God may be; He may not be. Therefore forgiveness from God is immaterial. It does not matter. All that matters is for men to forgive each other and relate properly. Forgiveness from an invisible, personal God is a far-fetched idea.

2. The attitude of the guilt- or conscience-stricken person. This is a person who knows little, if anything, about a personal God, yet he is deeply conscious of guilt and the need for forgiveness. He prays for forgiveness over and over, but he never comes to know forgiveness.

3. The attitude of the social religionist. This is a person who is sometimes mentally aware of the need for forgiveness; therefore, he makes an occasional confession. He feels forgiven, arises and goes about his affairs with no more thought about the matter. The problem with this is that it is a false forgiveness, a mental forgiveness. The person views God as a *patsy - grandfather* who allows a person to live like he wishes as long as he occasionally confesses. He ignores and denies the righteousness and justice of a loving God.

4. The attitude of the mature believer. This is a believer who truly knows his own sinful self and his great need for God's forgiveness. Therefore, he lives in a spirit of confession and repentance, by which he comes to know God's forgiveness and the assurance of it (see note—Ro.8:2-4).

---

1 (6:14) **Forgiveness of Others**: there is the promise to forgive and thereby to be forgiven. The word *trespass* (paraptoma) means to stumble; to fall; to slip; to blunder; to deviate from righteousness and truth. Note three things.

a. Christ takes for granted that we know that we need forgiveness. This is seen in His words, "your heavenly Father will also *forgive* you." We are sinners; we have transgressed God's law and we need forgiveness. Even the most mature among us fails to keep God's law perfectly. We all stumble, fall, blunder, and slip; and we do it much too often.

1) We are seldom doing to the fullest degree what we should do. We come short.

2) We are *always crossing over* from the path we should be following. We deviate over into *the forbidden* area. Thus, we desperately need forgiveness. God promises that He will forgive our trespasses if we will do one simple thing: forgive men their trespasses.

b. The greatest thing in all the world is to be forgiven our sins: to be absolved and released from all guilt and condemnation, to be accepted and restored by God and assured of seeing Christ face to face. Forgiveness of sins means that we are freed: set at liberty in this life to live abundantly, and set at liberty in the next life to live eternally in perfection.

c. The only way we can be forgiven our sins is to forgive others their trespasses. Christ makes the promise: "Forgive men their trespasses [and] your heavenly Father will also forgive you." Forgiving men their trespasses means several very practical things.

⇒ We are not judgmental or critical.
⇒ We do not become bitter or hostile.
⇒ We do not plan to take revenge.
⇒ We do not hold hard feelings against another person.
⇒ We do not talk about, gossip, or join in rumor; on the contrary, we correct the rumor.
⇒ We do not rejoice in trouble and trials that fall upon another person.
⇒ We love and pray for the person.

Thought 1. Note two facts.

(1) Bad feelings against another person is sin. It is holding sin within our heart. Forgiving a person who has done us evil is proof that we wish to have a clean heart. We really wish God to forgive us.

(2) Forgiving men their trespasses does not refer only to the trespasses against us, but all trespasses.

> **"Blessed are the merciful: for they shall obtain mercy" (Mt.5:7).**
> **"And when ye stand praying, forgive, if ye have ought against any: that your Father also which is in heaven may forgive you your trespasses" (Mk.11:25).**
> **"And forgive us our sins; for we also forgive every one that is indebted to us" (Lu.11:4).**
> **"And if he trespass against thee seven times in a day, and seven times in a day turn again to thee, saying, I repent; thou shalt forgive him" (Lu.17:4).**
> **"Forbearing one another, and forgiving one another, if any man have a quarrel against any: even as Christ forgave you, so also do ye" (Col.3:13).**

2 (6:15) **Forgiveness of Others**: there is the warning—refuse to forgive and be unforgiven. The believer who prays for forgiveness and holds feelings against another person is hypocritical. He is asking God to do something he himself is unwilling to do. He is asking God to forgive his trespasses when he himself is unwilling to forgive the trespasses of others. Bad feelings against a person are clear proof that a person is not right with God.

a. Bad feelings show that a person does not know the true nature of man nor of God. He does not know the true exalted perfection of God nor the real depth of man's sinful nature—how far short he is of perfect righteousness.

b. Bad feelings show that a person walks and lives in self-righteousness (that is, that he thinks that he is acceptable to God by deeds of righteousness). He feels better than others, and judges himself able to talk about and look askance at the sins of others.

c. Bad feelings show that a person has not taken the steps he must take in order to be forgiven his own sins (see DEEPER STUDY # 1, 2—Mt.6:14-15).

d. Bad feelings show that a person is living by the standards of society and not by God's Word. God's Word is clear: "there is none that doeth good, no, not one" (Ro.3:12; see Mt.19:17). Therefore, we are to help and love one another, to care for and restore one another when we stumble, slip, fall, blunder, and deviate.

> **"There is none righteous, no, not one" (Ro.3:10; see Ro.3:9-19).**
> **"All have sinned and come short of the glory of God" (Ro.3:23).**
> **"Let all bitterness, and wrath, and anger, and clamor [yelling, loud talk, loud threats], and evil speaking [talking about, rumor, gossip] be put away from you, with all malice: And be ye kind one to another, tenderhearted, forgiving one another, even as God for Christ's sake hath forgiven you" (Ep.4:31-32).**
> **"Brethren, if a man be overtaken in a fault, ye which are spiritual, restore such a one in the spirit of meekness; considering thyself, lest thou also be tempted. Bear ye one another's burdens, and so fulfill the law of Christ. For if a man think himself to be something, when he is nothing, he deceiveth himself" (Ga.6:1-3).**

Christ is explicitly clear in His warning about forgiving others.

> **"Be ye therefore merciful, as your Father also is merciful. Judge not, and ye shall not be judged: condemn not, and ye shall not be condemned: forgive, and ye shall be forgiven" (Lu.6:36-37).**

The warning is severe when the opposite statement is seen: Judge, and you will be judged; condemn, and you will be condemned; be unforgiving, and you will be unforgiven (see Lu.6:36-37).

Thought 1. Note three significant lessons in this point.

(1) The man who holds bad feelings against others has not looked at himself and his own sins. He does not know himself, not his real self, not the inner selfishness and motives that plague the depravity of man.

(2) Feelings against others cause inward disturbance. They eat away at a person's mind and emotions to varying degrees. Deep feelings against others can cause deep emotional and mental problems as well as serious physical problems.

(3) Three things are necessary for God to hear our prayer for forgiveness of sins. (1) Lifting up holy hands, (2) being without wrath, and (3) not doubting.

"I will therefore that men pray every where, lifting up holy hands, without wrath and doubting" (1 Ti.2:8).

Thought 2. The answer to inner peace is Christ Jesus. The answer to peace with others is also Christ. "He is our peace"—the only possible peace between two persons (see outline and notes—Ep.2:14-18. Review the Scriptures below verse by verse in light of the following facts.)

(1) He can make both one (Ep.2:14).
(2) He can break down the wall between both (Ep.2:14).
(3) He can abolish the enmity—in His own flesh (Ep.2:15).
(4) He can make the two into one new man (Ep.2:15).
(5) He can reconcile both to God—in one body—by the cross (Ep.2:15).
(6) He can give peace to both and bring peace between both (Ep.2:17).
(7) He can give both access to God the Father (Ep.2:18).

1. The wrong way to fast	P. The Right Motive for Fasting, 6:16-18	reward.	2. The right way to fast[DS1,2]
a. Fasting as a hypocrite	16 Moreover when ye fast, be not, as the hypocrites, of a sad countenance: for they disfigure their faces, that they may appear unto men to fast. Verily I say unto you, They have their	17 But thou, when thou fastest, anoint thine head, and wash thy face;	a. Fasting as a duty
		18 That thou appear not unto men to fast, but unto thy Father which is in secret: and thy Father, which seeth in secret, shall reward thee openly.	b. Fasting without notice
b. Fasting for recognition			c. Fasting for God alone
c. The reward: To receive only human recognition & esteem			d. The reward: God will reward the person who sincerely fasts in secret

DIVISION IV

THE TEACHINGS OF THE MESSIAH TO HIS DISCIPLES:
THE GREAT SERMON ON THE MOUNT, 5:1–7:29

P.   The Right Motive for Fasting, 6:16-18

(6:16-18) **Introduction—Fasting**: fasting means to abstain from food for some religious or spiritual purpose. A study of the fasting practiced by Jesus and by the great leaders of the Bible reveals what God means by fasting. Very simply, fasting means being so consumed with a matter that it becomes more important than food. Therefore, the believer sets food aside *in order to concentrate on seeking God about the matter*. Biblical fasting means more than just abstaining from food; it means to abstain from food in order to concentrate upon God and His answer to a particular matter. Biblical fasting involves prayer, intense supplication before God. Note the words "when ye fast" (vv.16, 17). Jesus assumed believers fasted; He expected them to fast. He fasted and He taught fasting (Mt.4:2), and the early believers fasted (Mt.17:21; Lu.2:37; Ac.10:30; 13:3; 14:23; 1 Co.7:5; 2 Co.6:5; 11:27). Yet so few have continued such intense seeking of the Lord: so few fast, truly fast.

The benefits of fasting are enormous, but there are also dangers. We can fast for the wrong reasons. This is the point of the present passage. Christ counsels us on the wrong and the right motives for fasting.

1. The wrong way to fast (v.16).
2. The right way to fast (vv.17-18).

1 (6:16) **Fasting**: the wrong way to fast.

a. Fasting as a hypocrite is wrong. Being hypocritical is a real danger when fasting. There are four reasons men fast, and all but one are false and hypocritical.
1) Men fast to gain a sense of God's approval and of self-approval.
2) Men fast to fulfill a religious act.
3) Men fast to gain religious recognition.
4) Men fast to genuinely meet God for some special purpose.

Thought 1. Fasting is not condemned by Christ. Fasting for any purpose other than to meet God is condemned: when you fast "appear...unto thy Father" (v.18).

"Therefore when thou doest thine alms, do not sound a trumpet before thee, as the hypocrites do in the synagogues and in the streets, that they may have glory of men. Verily I say unto you, They have their reward" (Mt.6:2).
"This people draweth nigh unto me with their mouth, and honoureth me with their lips; but their heart is far from me" (Mt.15:8).
"I fast twice in the week, I give tithes of all that I possess" (Lu.18:12).
"Having a form of godliness, but denying the power thereof: from such turn away" (2 Ti.3:5).
"Wherefore the Lord said, Forasmuch as this people draw near me with their mouth, and with their lips do honor me, but have removed their heart far from me, and their fear toward me is taught by the precept of men" (Is.29:13).
"For I desired mercy, and not sacrifice; and the knowledge of God more than burnt offerings" (Ho.6:6).

b. Fasting for recognition is wrong. It poses several serious dangers that must be guarded against with all diligence.
1) The danger of feeling super-spiritual. Few believers follow a true fast. Therefore when they really fast, they have to guard against a sense of super-spirituality and pride.
2) The danger of over-confidence. The believer's confidence is to be in God, not in self. After a genuine fast a believer usually feels spiritually confident, ready to go forth. He must go forth depending upon the strength of Christ and not upon his own energy and effort.
3) The danger of sharing one's fasting experience. The believer has usually learned so much from being in God's presence that he is anxious to share it, especially with those closest to him. The best advice is to hush: share nothing, not even with one's dearest friend.
4) The danger of changing one's appearance and the way one acts and behaves. Any change whatsoever from one's normal behavior and routine attracts attention and ruins the whole benefit of the fast. As Christ says, "they disfigure their faces" (act super-spiritual) (v.16).

23

"But all their works they do for to be seen of men" (Mt.23:5).

"Woe unto you, scribes and Pharisees, hypocrites! for ye are like unto whited sepulchres, which indeed appear beautiful outward, but are within full of dead men's bones, and of all uncleanness" (Mt.23:27).

"Judge not according to the appearance, but judge righteous judgment" (Jn.7:24).

"Do ye look on things after the outward appearance?" (2 Co.10:7).

c. Fasting the wrong way has its reward. A person will receive human recognition and esteem, but the recognition of men is all he will ever receive.

Thought 1. Some gain the control and discipline of their bodies through fasting, but they ruin themselves and their ministry through pride. They lose their reward.

"For all flesh is as grass, and all the glory of man as the flower of grass. The grass withereth, and the flower thereof falleth away" (1 Pe.1:24).

"Nevertheless man being in honour abideth not: he is like the beasts that perish" (Ps.49:12).

"For when he dieth he shall carry nothing away: his glory shall not descend after him" (Ps.49:17).

"Therefore hell hath enlarged herself, and opened her mouth without measure: and their glory, and their multitude, and their pomp, and he that rejoiceth, shall descend into it" (Is.5:14).

"As they were increased, so they sinned against me: therefore will I change their glory into shame" (Ho.4:7).

2 (6:17-18) **Fasting**: the right way to fast. As stated in the introduction, fasting means being so consumed with a matter that it becomes more important than food. Therefore, the believer sets food aside *in order to concentrate on seeking* God about the matter. Biblical fasting means more than just abstaining from food; it means to abstain from food in order to concentrate upon God and His answer to a particular matter. Biblical fasting involves prayer, intense supplication before God.

a. Fasting is a duty. Every believer is expected to fast. Christ said "When ye fast" (v.16). He expects us to fast.

⇒ Jesus Himself fasted.

"And when he had fasted forty days and forty nights, he was afterward an hungred" (Mt.4:2).

⇒ The apostles were to fast.

"Howbeit this kind goeth not out but by prayer and fasting" (Mt.17:21; see Mt.9:15; Mk.2:20; Lu.5:35).

⇒ Anna fasted.

"And she was a widow of about fourscore and four years, which departed not from the temple, but served God with fastings and prayers night and day" (Lu.2:37).

⇒ Cornelius fasted.

"And Cornelius said, Four days ago I was fasting until this hour; and at the ninth hour I prayed in my house, and, behold, a man stood before me in bright clothing" (Ac.10:30).

⇒ Church leaders fasted.

"As they ministered to the Lord, and fasted, the Holy Ghost said, Separate me Barnabas and Saul for the work whereunto I have called them" (Ac.13:2).

"And when they had ordained them elders in every church, and had prayed with fasting, they commended them to the Lord, on whom they believed" (Ac.14:23).

⇒ Husbands and wives are expected to fast.

"Defraud ye not [do not deprive] one the other, except it be with consent for a time, that ye may give yourselves to *fasting* and prayer; and come together again, that Satan tempt you not for your incontinency" (1 Co.7:5).

⇒ Paul fasted often.

"In stripes, in imprisonments, in tumults, in labours, in watchings, in fastings; by pureness, by knowledge, by longsuffering, by kindness, by the Holy Ghost, by love unfeigned" (2 Co.6:5).

"In weariness and painfulness, in watchings often, in hunger and thirst, in fastings often, in cold and nakedness" (2 Co.11:27).

b. Fasting is to be done without notice. The believer is to fast before God, not before men. There is to be no change in appearance or behavior to indicate that he is fasting. Think about it. Why should there be? Why should anyone know that a person is seeking God in a very special way? The matter is God's affair, not man's affair. It is between the person and God, not the person and other people.

Thought 1. What is fasting? It is to "appear not unto men...but unto thy Father" (v.18). It is to come into God's presence for a very, very special session of prayer.

c. Fasting is to be to God alone. The believer is to fast to God alone. God is the object of his fast. He needs to meet God in a very, very special way. In meeting God all alone, the believer is demonstrating his dependency upon God and His provision. (See note—Mt.6:16-18.)

Thought 1. A religionist fasts before men. A genuine believer fasts before God.

Thought 2. God does not say when nor how often we should fast, but He does tell us how to fast. We must take every precaution to fast exactly as He says: before God, in secret, without any ostentation or show whatsoever. No one is to see or know.

d. Fasting the right way has its reward: God shall reward us openly. How much greater is His reward than the recognition of men! God's acceptance and eternal reward is enough for genuine believers.

"But when thou doest alms, let not thy left hand know what thy right hand doeth: that thine alms may be in secret: and thy Father which seeth in secret himself shall reward thee openly" (Mt.6:3-4).
"For we must all [publicly, before all believers] appear before the judgment seat of Christ; that every one may receive the things done in his body, according to that he hath done, whether it be good or bad" (2 Co.5:10).
"Look to yourselves, that we lose not those things which we have wrought, but that we receive a full reward" (2 Jn.8).
"And, behold, I come quickly; and my reward is with me, to give every man according as his work shall be" (Re.22:12).
"The judgments of the Lord are true and righteous altogether....Moreover by them is thy servant warned: and in keeping of them there is great reward" (Ps.19:9, 11).
"So that a man shall say, Verily there is a reward for the righteous: verily he is a God that judgeth in the earth" (Ps.58:11).
"Behold, the Lord GOD will come with strong hand, and his arm shall rule for him: behold, his reward is with him, and his work before him" (Is.40:10).
"Behold, the Lord hath proclaimed unto the end of the world, Say ye to the daughter of Zion, Behold, thy salvation cometh; behold, his reward is with him, and his work before him" (Is.62:11).
"I the LORD search the heart, I try the reins, even to give every man according to his ways, and according to the fruit of his doings" (Je.17:10).
"Can any hide himself in secret places that I shall not see him? saith the LORD. Do not I fill heaven and earth? saith the LORD" (Je.23:24).

DEEPER STUDY # 1
(6:17-18) **Fasting**: there are at least four times when the believer should fast.
1. There are times when the believer feels a special pull, an urge, a call within his heart to get alone with God. This is God's Spirit moving within his heart. When this happens, nothing—not food, not responsibility—should keep him from getting all alone with God. He should fast as soon as possible.
2. There are times when special needs arise. The needs may concern the believer's own life or the life of friends, society, the world, or some ministry or mission. Again, nothing should keep the believer from spending a very special time in God's presence when facing such dire needs.
3. There are times when the believer needs to humble his soul before God. At such times he learns not only humility but dependence upon God (Ps.35:13).
4. There are times when the believer needs a very special power from God. The Lord promised such power if the believer prayed and fasted (Mt.17:21; Mk.9:29).

DEEPER STUDY # 2
(6:17-18) **Fasting**: Why are believers to fast? There are excellent benefits to fasting, and God wants His people to reap these benefits.
1. Fasting keeps the believer in the presence of God. He is fasting in order to seek God's presence for a very special purpose; he remains in God's presence until he feels God has or is going to meet his need.
2. Fasting humbles the believer's soul before God. It says that God is the most important thing in all the world to him (Ps.35:13).
3. Fasting teaches the believer his dependency upon God. He is seeking God, and in so doing he is demonstrating his conviction that he is dependent upon God.
4. Fasting demonstrates to God (by action) a real seriousness. It shows by act that the matter being considered is a priority.
5. Fasting teaches the believer to control and discipline his life. He does without in order to gain a greater substance.
6. Fasting keeps the believer from being enslaved by habit. He lays aside all substances; in so doing, he breaks the hold of anything that might have him chained.
7. Fasting helps the believer to stay physically fit. It helps keep him from becoming overweight and soft.

	Q. The Warning About Wealth & Materialism, 6:19-24	22 The light of the body is the eye: if therefore thine eye be single, thy whole body shall be full of light.	eye 1) Focuses & sees 2) Focuses on heaven, v. 20

1. A contrast: Between two kinds of riches
  a. Earthly riches
    1) Are not to be laid up
    2) Are corruptible*DS1*
    3) Are insecure
  b. Heavenly riches
    1) Are to be laid up
    2) Are indestructible
    3) Are secure
2. A warning: About two kinds of hearts
  a. A good heart: Like a good
	19 Lay not up for yourselves treasures upon earth, where moth and rust doth corrupt, and where thieves break through and steal:
	20 But lay up for yourselves treasures in heaven, where neither moth nor rust doth corrupt, and where thieves do not break through nor steal:
	21 For where your treasure is, there will your heart be also.
		23 But if thine eye be evil, thy whole body shall be full of darkness. If therefore the light that is in thee be darkness, how great *is* that darkness!
		24 No man can serve two masters: for either he will hate the one, and love the other; or else he will hold to the one, and despise the other. Ye cannot serve God and mammon.
			b. A bad heart: Like a bad eye
			  1) Is blind & dark
			  2) Focuses on the earth, v. 19
			
			3. A choice: Between two kinds of masters
			  a. Will either hate the one & love the other
			  b. Will either cling to the one & despise the other
			  c. The choice: Cannot serve God & material things*DS2*

DIVISION IV

THE TEACHINGS OF THE MESSIAH TO HIS DISCIPLES:
THE GREAT SERMON ON THE MOUNT, 5:1–7:29

Q. The Warning About Wealth and Materialism, 6:19-24

(6:19-24) **Introduction**: Where are our thoughts? What do we think about? Are our thoughts on earth or on heaven? Is our mind on earthly things or on God? What are we seeking, the things of the earth or the things of heaven? Where is our heart, focused on earth or focused on heaven? The concern of Christ in this passage is money, possessions, and material things. His concern is that we guard against centering our lives around houses, furnishings, cars, lands, buildings, stocks—all the things that make up security and wealth on this earth. The reason is simply understood: nothing on this earth is secure and lasting. It is aging, decaying, and wasting away. It is all corruptible and temporal. What Christ wants is for us to center our lives around Him and heaven, for everything about Himself and heaven is life and security. It is all permanent and eternal. To stir our thinking He gives us a lesson on wealth and materialism. (Also see outline and DEEPER STUDY # 3—Mt.13:7, 22.)

    1. A contrast: between two kinds of riches (vv.19-20).
    2. A warning: about two kinds of hearts (vv.21-23).
    3. A choice: between two kinds of masters (v.24).

1 (6:19-20) **Materialism—Wealth**: Christ gives a contrast about two kinds of riches.

a. There are earthly riches. There are things on earth that men desire. Christ calls these earthly riches and treasures. Earthly riches would be such things as clothes, cars, jewelry, toys, houses, buildings, furnishings, pleasure, fame, power, profession, property, money—anything that dominates a person's life and holds it fast to this earth.

A treasure is that which has value and is worth something to someone. Men take things and ascribe value to them: it may be stones (diamonds); or rocks and dust (gold); or money (paper and metal); or land (property); or wood, metal, dirt, chemical, and fabric (buildings); or influence (power); or the attention of people (fame).

Christ says three things about earthly riches that are of critical importance to both the believer and the unbeliever.

    1) Do not lay up for yourselves earthly riches (material possessions). Christ says that a person is not to focus his life on earthly things, not to set his eyes and mind and energy and effort on such passing treasures.

    Thought 1. Riches do exist. And their *locality* is clearly stated. There is wealth both on *earth* and in *heaven*.

    Thought 2. It is easier to covet earthly things than heavenly things for four reasons.
    (1) They are seen and can be handled.
    (2) They are sought by most people, and other people influence us. A person is either worldly minded or heavenly minded (Ro.8:5-7).
    (3) They are to varying degrees necessary for life.
    (4) They are present, ever before us, and can be possessed right now.

    2) Earthly riches are corruptible (see DEEPER STUDY # 1—Mt.6:19). Something terrible happens to everything on earth. Everything ages, dies, deteriorates, and decays. Things are on the earth only for a brief time, and then they are no more. Everything has the seed of corruption within it.

    3) Earthly riches are insecure. The things on earth are insecure for three reasons.
    ⇒ They can be stolen or eaten up.
    ⇒ They do not last; they waste away.
    ⇒ A person cannot take a single thing with him when he passes from this world.

"For we brought nothing into this world, and it is certain we can carry nothing out" (1 Ti.6:7).

"For the love of money is the root of all evil: which while some coveted after, they have erred from the faith, and pierced themselves through with many sorrows"
(1 Ti.6:10).

"Your gold and silver is cankered; and the rust of them shall be a witness against you, and shall eat your flesh as it were fire. Ye have heaped treasure together for the last days" (Js.5:3).

"The increase of his house shall depart, and his goods shall flow away in the day of his wrath" (Jb.20:28).

"Surely every man walketh in a vain show; surely they are disquieted in vain: he heapeth up riches, and knoweth not who shall gather them" (Ps.39:6).

"For he seeth that wise men die, likewise the fool and the brutish person perish, and leave their wealth to others" (Ps.49:10).

"Wilt thou set thine eyes upon that which is not? for riches certainly make themselves wings; they fly away as an eagle toward heaven" (Pr.23:5).

"For riches are not for ever: and doth the crown endure to every generation?" (Pr.27:24).

"Yea, I hated all my labor which I had taken under the sun: because I should leave it unto the man that shall be after me" (Ec.2:18).

"He that loveth silver shall not be satisfied with silver; nor he that loveth abundance with increase: this is also vanity" (Ec.5:10).

"As the partridge sitteth on eggs, and hatcheth them not; so he that getteth riches, and not by right, shall leave them in the midst of his days, and at his end shall be a fool" (Je.17:11).

"With thy wisdom and with thine understanding thou hast gotten thee riches, and hast gotten gold and silver into thy treasures: by thy great wisdom and by thy traffic hast thou increased thy riches, and thine heart is lifted up because of thy riches" (Eze.28:4-5).

Thought 1. Note four striking lessons.
(1) Wealth is sought, and it is sought by many. What is often forgotten is this: every bit of wealth is held by someone. Therefore, many are always figuring how to get some of what someone else has. Things of the world are very insecure.
(2) A man can be snatched away from this earth as quickly as the twinkling of an eye. Everything for which he has worked so hard on this earth can be gone immediately (see Lu.12:16-21).
(3) A man can lose much of what he has in this world and lose it quickly. He can lose it through financial difficulties, accident, marital problems, illness, death, and a myriad of other ways.
(4) A person is a fool to seek an abundance of things—to grasp after more and more. Why? Because tonight or tomorrow or some day soon God will say, "Thou fool, this night thy soul shall be required of thee: then whose shall these things be, which thou hast provided?" (Lu.12:20).
Christ says, "He that layeth up treasure for himself, and is not rich toward God"—is going to hear the above (Lu.12:21).

b. There are heavenly riches. There are things in heaven that believers desire. Christ calls these heavenly riches (see outline and notes—Ep.1:3 for the list of God's heavenly blessings). Heavenly riches would be such things as...
- a blameless life
- becoming a true child of God
- the forgiveness of sins
- wisdom
- understanding the will of God (purpose, meaning, and significance in life)
- an enormous inheritance that is eternal
- a constant Comforter and Helper, the Holy Spirit of God Himself
- life that is abundant and overflowing (Jn.10:10)

Christ says three things about heavenly riches that are of critical importance to the believer and the unbeliever.
1) Lay up for yourselves heavenly riches. A person is foolish to seek and set his mind on perishable things. Why? Because he can seek after that which gives all the meaning, purpose, and significance to life that one can imagine. To have meaning and purpose and significance in life is what life is all about.
   Think about it. "A man's life consisteth not in the abundance of things which he possesseth" (Lu.12:15). How much meaning is there in something that passes and perishes? Even while a person seeks after something on this earth, there is an inner awareness that it will not last. There is an end to whatever meaning he finds in it. The earthly treasure may be a car, a job, a trip, a relationship, clothing, position, power, fame, or fortune. The fact is, no matter what the treasure is, it will end and pass away and be no more. A worldly man's meaning for living, his purpose and significance in life, is temporary, unfulfilling and incomplete. (See note 4 and DEEPER STUDY # 1—Ep.1:7; note 5 and DEEPER STUDY # 1—2 Pe.1:4; see Ep.1:3.)
2) Heavenly riches are incorruptible. Corruption can be escaped (2 Pe.1:4). There is an "inheritance incorruptible, and undefiled, and that fadeth not away, *reserved in heaven for you*" (1 Pe.1:4). Everyone should lay claim and set his heart on *his* heavenly inheritance.
3) Heavenly riches are secure (see notes—Ep.1:3). Thieves cannot break through heaven; they cannot penetrate the spiritual dimension. No one nor anything can take away a person's heavenly riches. The love of God assures this (see Ro.8:32-39).

Thought 1. Christ does not stop a man from seeking treasure; contrariwise, He guides the man's search to real treasure. Heaven is worth more than all the wealth in the world.

⇒ "For what is a man profited, if he shall gain the whole world, and lose his own soul? or what shall a man give in exchange for his soul?" (Mt.16:26).

⇒ "For what shall it profit a man, if he shall gain the whole world, and lose his own soul?" (Mk.8:36).

⇒ "For what is a man advantaged, if he gain the whole world, and lose himself, or be cast away?" (Lu.9:25).

Thought 2. A man must leave all to follow Christ or else he cannot be the Lord's disciple.

"So likewise, whosoever he be of you that forsaketh not all that he hath, he cannot be my disciple" (Lu.14:33).

Thought 3. Christ says a man is to lay up treasures in heaven for himself, not lay up treasures on earth for his family. A pointed and disturbing message to many!

"But lay up for yourselves treasures in heaven, where neither moth nor rust doth corrupt, and where thieves do not break through nor steal" (Mt.6:20).

"Jesus said unto him. If thou wilt be perfect, go and sell that thou hast, and give to the poor, and thou shalt have treasure in heaven: and come and follow me" (Mt.19:21).

"Sell that ye have, and give alms; provide yourselves bags which wax not old, a treasure in the heavens that faileth not" (Lu.12:33).

"Yea doubtless, and I count all things but loss for the excellency of the knowledge of Christ Jesus my Lord: for whom I suffered the loss of all things, and do count them but dung, that I may win Christ" (Ph.3:8).

"Laying up in store for themselves a good foundation against the time to come, that they may lay hold on eternal life" (1 Ti.6:19).

"I counsel thee to buy of me gold tried in the fire, that thou mayest be rich; and white raiment, that thou mayest be clothed, and that the shame of thy nakedness do not appear; and anoint thine eyes with eyesalve, that thou mayest see" (Re.3:18).

DEEPER STUDY # 1

(6:19) **Corruption—Incorruption**: there is a seed of corruption within the world—a principle or nature of corruption within everything on earth. Everything is imperfectly born and formed; it ages, dies, deteriorates, decays, and wastes away. (See DEEPER STUDY # 2—Mt.8:17; notes—1 Co.15:50; 2 Co.5:1-4; Col.2:8; note 5 and DEEPER STUDY # 1—2 Pe.1:4.)

"That it might be fulfilled which was spoken by Esaias the prophet, saying, Himself took our infirmities, and bare our sicknesses" (Mt.8:17).

"Now this I say, brethren, that flesh and blood cannot inherit the kingdom of God; neither doth corruption inherit incorruption" (1 Co.15:50).

"For we know that if our earthly house of this tabernacle were dissolved, we have a building of God, an house not made with hands, eternal in the heavens....If so be that being clothed we shall not be found naked" (2 Co.5:1, 3).

"Whereby are given unto us exceeding great and precious promises: that by these ye might be partakers of the divine nature, having escaped the corruption that is in the world through lust" (2 Pe.1:4).

There is also a seed of incorruption, a principle of incorruption, an eternal nature of incorruption in heaven (1 Pe.1:4, 23; see 1:18-23; 2 Pe.1:4; see 1 Co.15:12-58. See note—Ep.1:3.)

"Blessed be the God and Father of our Lord Jesus Christ, which according to his abundant mercy hath begotten us again unto a lively hope by the resurrection of Jesus Christ from the dead, to an inheritance incorruptible, and undefiled, and that fadeth not away, reserved in heaven for you" (1 Pe.1:3-4).

"Being born again, not of corruptible seed, but of incorruptible, by the word of God, which liveth and abideth for ever" (1 Pe.1:23).

"So also is the resurrection of the dead. It is sown in corruption; it is raised in incorruption: it is sown in dishonour; it is raised in glory: it is sown in weakness; it is raised in power: it is sown a natural body: it is raised a spiritual body. There is a natural body, and there is a spiritual body" (1 Co.15:42-44; see 1 Co.15:12-58).

---

2 (6:21-23) **Heart—Mind**: Christ warns about two kinds of hearts.

a. There is the good heart. It is just like a good eye. Note that the eye is a gate that *gives entrance* to the mind of man. What man looks at is what he thinks about, and what he thinks about is what he actually becomes (see Pr.23:7). If a man focuses upon Jesus Christ, who is the Light of the world (Jn.8:12), then his mind and heart will be *full of light*. Therefore, the deeds of his body will be deeds of light. Singleness of the eye and heart means that a person sets his attention upon the Lord Jesus for the purpose of doing His will (see Ac.2:46; Ep.6:5; Col.3:22). An evil eye is one that focuses upon anything that is not of God.

A man's heart is precisely where his treasure is. If his treasure is on earth, his heart is on earth. If his treasure is in heaven, his heart is in heaven. The eye illustrates the truth. If a man's eye is *good and healthy*, then he is able to focus upon the treasure and grasp the truth. But if the eye is *unhealthy*, he is not able to focus upon the treasure. He is blind and in darkness. A *healthy heart* is like a healthy eye. It grasps the true treasure, the treasure in heaven. But an *unhealthy heart* is like an unhealthy eye. It is in darkness, unable to see the treasure in heaven.

Note that the believer fixes his eyes upon heaven for two primary reasons.

1) His citizenship is in heaven:

> **"For our conversation [citizenship] is in heaven; from whence also we look for the Savior, the Lord Jesus Christ: who shall change our vile body, that it may be fashioned like unto His glorious body" (Ph.3:20-21).**

2) He seeks the treasures which are eternal:

> **"For the things which are seen are temporal; but the things which are not seen are eternal" (2 Co.4:18).**

⇒ They are incorruptible (v.20).
⇒ They are secure (v.20).
⇒ They cause his "whole body to be full of light" (v.22).
⇒ They consume his whole being in all the meaning and purpose and significance of life (v.24).
⇒ They cause him to love and to serve God (v.24).
⇒ They draw him near to God (v.24).

> **"Blessed are the pure in heart: for they shall see God" (Mt.5:8).**
> **"Then spake Jesus again unto them, saying, I am the light of the world: he that followeth me shall not walk in darkness, but shall have the light of life" (Jn.8:12).**
> **"Yet a little while, and the world seeth me no more; but ye see me: because I live, ye shall live also" (Jn.14:19).**
> **"But the natural man receiveth not the things of the Spirit of God: for they are foolishness unto him: neither can he know them, because they are spiritually discerned" (1 Co.2:14).**
> **"By faith he forsook Egypt, not fearing the wrath of the king: for he endured, as seeing him who is invisible" (He.11:27).**

Thought 1. The believer has a clear cut charge: "Set your affection on things above, not in things on the earth" (Col.3:2).

> **"Blessed be the God and Father of our Lord Jesus Christ, who hath blessed us with all spiritual blessings in heavenly places in Christ" (Ep.1:3).**
> **"The eyes of your understanding being enlightened; that ye may know what is the hope of his calling, and what the riches of the glory of his inheritance in the saints" (Ep.1:18).**
> **"Unto me, who am less than the least of all saints, is this grace given, that I should preach among the Gentiles the unsearchable riches of Christ" (Ep.3:8).**
> **"[Moses] esteeming the reproach of Christ greater riches than the treasures in Egypt: for he had respect unto the recompense of the reward" (He.11:26).**
> **"Hearken, my beloved brethren, Hath not God chosen the poor of this world rich in faith, and heirs of the kingdom which he hath promised to them that love him?" (Js.2:5).**

b. There is the bad heart. It is just like a bad eye. A bad eye is not able to focus upon the treasure, not able to focus upon the things of God. A bad eye is blind and in darkness. So it is with the heart. Christ says that a person is not to set his heart upon earthly treasures. Why? Such a person focuses his eyes (attention, mind, thoughts, energy, effort) on evil. What does Christ mean? Earthly things are evil because they are deceiving.

⇒ They are corruptible; they age, die, waste away, deteriorate, and decay (v.19).
⇒ They are insecure; they will be stolen or taken away or left behind (v.19).
⇒ They cause a person's heart to be full of darkness (v.23).
⇒ They will consume a person (v.24).
⇒ They cause a person to hate, despise, and reject God (v.24).
⇒ They alienate a person from God (v.24).

Thought 1. Several things happen to a man who sets his eye upon earthly things. The shadows of darkness set in upon him. He becomes deceived (see Mt.13:7, 22). He is deceived in that he becomes...
• covetous and consuming (to get more and more)
• complaining and grudging
• apprehensive and fearful (of losing it)
• hard and close-minded (to giving much). (See Js.5:9).

> **"But if thine eye be evil, thy whole body shall be full of darkness. If therefore the light that is in thee be darkness, how great is that darkness!" (Mt.6:23).**
> **"And the light shineth in darkness; and the darkness comprehended it not" (Jn.1:5).**

"And this is the condemnation, that light is come into the world, and men loved darkness rather than light, because their deeds were evil" (Jn.3:19).

"In whom the God of this world hath blinded the minds of them which believe not, lest the light of the glorious gospel of Christ, who is the image of God, should shine unto them" (2 Co.4:4).

"Having the understanding darknened, being alienated from the life of God through the ignorance that is in them, because of the blindness of their heart" (Ep.4:18).

3 (6:24) **Decision**: Christ warns that a choice has to be made between two kinds of masters. There are two critical reasons why a choice has to be made.

a. A man hates one master and loves the other. When both masters call upon the man at the same time, he has to make a choice. He favors, serves, helps, and loves one; and while he is doing so, he is disfavoring, rejecting, and showing disrespect and hate for the other. A man cannot serve two masters.

b. A man either cleaves to or despises one of the masters. He has to choose which master to favor and serve. He has to cleave to one. In cleaving to one, he reveals disrespect and spite for the other. A man cannot serve two masters.

The choice is clear. A man either serves God or material things.

⇒ There are only two treasures: the earth and its treasures or God and His treasures, physical and material things or spiritual and eternal things.

⇒ Every man without exception has committed his life to one of two treasures: mammon or God. He is focusing his heart, eyes, mind, attention, thoughts, hands, and energy upon earthly things or upon heavenly things. He cannot "serve God *and* mammon."

Thought 1. So many look at wealth as a blessing of God, a sign that one is godly. But the Bible says differently.

"[Some] suppose that gain is godliness: from such withdraw thyself. But godliness with contentment is great gain. For we brought nothing into this world, and it is certain we can carry nothing out. And having food and raiment let us be therewith content. But they that will be rich fall into temptation and a snare, and into many foolish and hurtful lusts, which drown men in destruction and perdition. For the love of money is the root of all evil: which while some coveted after, they have erred from the faith, and pierced themselves through with many sorrows. But thou, O man of God, flee these things: and follow after righteousness, godliness, faith, love, patience, meekness" (1 Ti.6:5-11).

Thought 2. Mammon, earthly treasures, can be many things (see Mt.6:19-20).
(1) Riches and wealth.

"Go to now, ye that say, To day or to morrow we will go into such a city, and continue there a year, and buy and sell, and get gain" (Js.4:13).

"Go to now, ye rich men, weep and howl for your miseries that shall come upon you" (Js.5:1).

(2) Food, the filling of one's belly.

"Whose end is destruction, whose God is their belly, and whose glory is in their shame, who mind earthly things" (Ph.3:19).

(3) An evil, lusting eye.

"But I say unto you, That whosoever looketh on a woman to lust after her hath committed adultery with her already in his heart" (Mt.5:28).

"But if thine eye be evil, thy whole body shall be full of darkness. If therefore the light that is in thee be darkness, how great is that darkness!" (Mt.6:23).

"Thefts, covetousness, wickedness, deceit, lasciviousness, an evil eye, blasphemy, pride, foolishness" (Mk.7:22).

(4) A lusting of the flesh.

"Love not the world, neither the things that are in the world. If any man love the world, the love of the Father is not in him. For all that is in the world, the lust of the flesh, and the lust of the eyes, and the pride of life, is not of the Father, but is of the world" (1 Jn.2:15-16).

(5) Unproductive activity, relaxation, recreation, wasteful pastimes, sluggish feelings.

"Go to the ant, thou sluggard; consider her ways, and be wise: which having no guide, overseer, or ruler, provideth her meat in the summer, and gathereth her food in the harvest. How long wilt thou sleep, O sluggard? when wilt thou arise out of thy sleep? Yet a little sleep, a little slumber, a little folding of the hands to sleep: so shall thy poverty come as one that travelleth, and thy want as an armed man" (Pr.6:6-11).

Thought 3. God promises several great things to the man who serves Him.
(1) All the necessities of life.

> **"But seek ye first the kingdom of God, and his righteousness; and all these things shall be added unto you" (Mt.6:33).**

(2) Freedom from anxiety.

> **"Be careful for nothing; but in every thing by prayer and supplication with thanksgiving let your requests be made known unto God. And the peace of God, which passeth all understanding, shall keep your hearts and minds through Christ Jesus" (Ph.4:6-7).**

(3) Joy and contentment.

> **"These things have I spoken unto you, that my joy might remain in you, and that your joy might be full" (Jn.15:11).**
> **"Let your conversation [behavior] be without covetousness; and be content with such things as ye have: for he hath said, I will never leave thee, nor forsake thee" (He.13:5).**

(4) Abundant and eternal life.

> **"For God so loved the world, that he gave his only begotten Son, that whosoever believeth in him should not perish, but have everlasting life" (Jn.3:16).**
> **"Verily, verily, I say unto you, He that heareth my word, and beliveth on him that sent me, hath everlasting life, and shall not come into condemnation; but is passed from death unto life" (Jn.5:24).**
> **"I am come that they might have life, and that they might have it more abundantly" (Jn.10:10).**

DEEPER STUDY # 2
(6:24) **Wealth:** see DEEPER STUDY # 1—Mt.19:16-22; notes—19:23-26; 19:27-30; pt.2 Js.1:9-11.

OUTLINE BIBLE RESOURCES

This material, like similar works, has come from imperfect man and is thus susceptible to human error. We are nevertheless grateful to God for both calling us and empowering us through His Holy Spirit to undertake this task. Because of His goodness and grace, *The Preacher's Outline & Sermon Bible*® New Testament is complete and the Old Testament volumes are releasing periodically.

The Minister's Personal Handbook and other helpful **Outline Bible Resources** are available in printed form as well as releasing electronically on WORDsearch software.

God has given the strength and stamina to bring us this far. Our confidence is that as we keep our eyes on Him and grounded in the undeniable truths of the Word, we will continue working through the Old Testament volumes. The future includes other helpful Outline Bible Resources for God's dear servants to use in their Bible Study and discipleship.

We offer this material first to Him in whose Name we labor and serve and for whose glory it has been produced and, second, to everyone everywhere who preaches and teaches the Word.

Our daily prayer is that each volume will lead thousands, millions, yes even billions, into a better understanding of the Holy Scriptures and a fuller knowledge of Jesus Christ the Incarnate Word, of whom the Scriptures so faithfully testify.

You will be pleased to know that Leadership Ministries Worldwide partners with Christian organizations, printers, and mission groups around the world to make Outline Bible Resources available and affordable in many countries and foreign languages. It is our goal that *every* leader around the world, both clergy and lay, will be able to understand God's Holy Word and present God's message with more clarity, authority, and understanding—all beyond his or her own power.

LEADERSHIP MINISTRIES WORLDWIDE
PO Box 21310 • Chattanooga, TN 37424-0310
423) 855-2181 • FAX (423) 855-8616
info@lmw.org
www.lmw.org - FREE Download materials

LEADERSHIP MINISTRIES WORLDWIDE

Publishers of Outline Bible Resources

OBR

- ### THE PREACHER'S OUTLINE & SERMON BIBLE® (POSB) • KJV – NIV

NEW TESTAMENT

Matthew 1 (chapters 1–15)
Matthew 2 (chapters 16–28)
Mark
Luke
John
Acts
Romans

1 & 2 Corinthians
Galatians, Ephesians, Philippians, Colossians
1 & 2 Thessalonians, 1 & 2 Timothy, Titus, Philemon
Hebrews, James
1 & 2 Peter, 1, 2, & 3 John, Jude
Revelation
Master Outline & Subject Index

OLD TESTAMENT

Genesis 1 (chapters 1–11)
Genesis 2 (chapters 12–50)
Exodus 1 (chapters 1–18)
Exodus 2 (chapters 19–40)
Leviticus
Numbers
Deuteronomy
Joshua
Judges, Ruth
1 Samuel
2 Samuel

1 Kings
2 Kings
1 Chronicles
2 Chronicles
Ezra, Nehemiah, Esther, Job
Psalms 1 (chapters 1-41)
Psalms 2 (chapters 42-106)
Psalms 3 (chapters 107-150)
Proverbs
Ecclesiastes, Song of Solomon

Isaiah 1 (chapters 1-35)
Isaiah 2 (chapters 36-66)
Jeremiah 1 (chapters 1-29)
Jeremiah 2 (chapters 30-52),
 Lamentations
Ezekiel
Daniel, Hosea
Joel, Amos, Obadiah, Jonah,
 Micah, Nahum
Habakkuk, Zephaniah, Haggai,
 Zechariah, Malachi

Print versions of all Outline Bible Resources are available in various forms.

- *What the Bible Says to the Believer* — **The Believer's Personal Handbook**
  11 Chs. – Over 500 Subjects, 300 Promises, & 400 Verses Expounded - Italian Imitation Leather or Paperback
- *What the Bible Says to the Minister* — **The Minister's Personal Handbook**
  12 Chs. - 127 Subjects - 400 Verses Expounded - Italian Imitation Leather or Paperback
- **Practical Word Studies In the New Testament** — 2 Vol. Hardcover Set
- **The Teacher's Outline & Study Bible™ - Various New Testament Books**
  Complete 30 - 45 minute lessons – with illustrations and discussion questions
- **Practical Illustrations — Companion to the POSB**
  Arranged by topic and Scripture reference
- **What the Bible Says About Series – Various Subjects**
- **OBR on various digital platforms**
  See current digital providers on our website at www.lmw.org
- **Non-English Translations of various books**
  See our website for more information or contact our office

— Contact LMW for quantity orders and information —

LEADERSHIP MINISTRIES WORLDWIDE or Your Local Christian Bookstore
PO Box 21310 • Chattanooga, TN 37424-0310
(423) 855-2181 • FAX (423) 855-8616 (Mon. - Thurs. 9am – 5pm Eastern)
E-mail - info@lmw.org • Order online at www.lmw.org

PURPOSE STATEMENT

LEADERSHIP MINISTRIES WORLDWIDE

exists to equip ministers, teachers, and laymen in their understanding, preaching, and teaching of God's Word by publishing and distributing worldwide *The Preacher's Outline & Sermon Bible®* and related **Outline Bible Resources**; to reach & disciple men, women, boys and girls for Jesus Christ.

MISSION STATEMENT

1. To make the Bible so understandable – its truth so clear and plain – that men and women everywhere, whether teacher or student, preacher or hearer, can grasp its message and receive Jesus Christ as Savior, and...

2. To place the Bible in the hands of all who will preach and teach God's Holy Word, verse by verse, precept by precept, regardless of the individual's ability to purchase it.

The **Outline Bible Resources** have been given to LMW for printing and especially distribution worldwide at/below cost, by those who remain anonymous. One fact, however, is as true today as it was in the time of Christ:

THE GOSPEL IS FREE, BUT THE COST OF TAKING IT IS NOT

LMW depends on the generous gifts of believers with a heart for Him and a love for the lost. They help pay for the printing, translating, and distributing of **Outline Bible Resources** into the hands of God's servants worldwide, who will present the Gospel message with clarity, authority, and understanding beyond their own.

LMW was incorporated in the state of Tennessee in July 1992 and received IRS 501 (c)(3) nonprofit status in March 1994. LMW is an international, nondenominational mission organization. All proceeds from USA sales, along with donations from donor partners, go directly to underwrite our translation and distribution projects of **Outline Bible Resources** to preachers, church and lay leaders, and Bible students around the world.

www.ingramcontent.com/pod-product-compliance
Lightning Source LLC
Chambersburg PA
CBHW081232020426
42331CB00012B/3145